One-M
Stress
Management

A Clinically Proven Programme
for Safeguarding Your Health and
Happiness in Sixty Seconds a Day

DAVID LEWIS

CEDAR

A Mandarin Paperback
ONE-MINUTE STRESS MANAGEMENT

First published in Great Britain 1993
in Cedar
by Mandarin Paperbacks
an imprint of Reed Consumer Books Limited
Michelin House, 81 Fulham Road, London SW3 6RB
and Auckland, Melbourne, Singapore and Toronto

Reprinted 1993 (twice), 1994

Copyright © 1993 by David Lewis
The author has asserted his moral rights

A CIP catalogue record for this title
is available from the British Library
ISBN 0 7493 1214 9

Phototypeset by Intype, London
Printed and bound in Great Britain
by Cox & Wyman Ltd, Reading, Berkshire

Should you read this book?

Try these two simple tests and then decide . . .

TEST ONE Clench your right hand.
Question Did you hold your breath while doing so?

TEST TWO Note the time. Now, without looking at your watch, estimate when sixty seconds have passed.
Question Did you *underestimate* by ten seconds or more?

If you answered yes to either of these questions, stress is causing you distress.

In this book I will explain how to make stress work for rather than against you. By mastering these quick and easy-to-use procedures you will be able to transform a potentially destructive force into a powerful ally, liberating hidden reserves of creative energy and enabling you to lead a happier, healthier and more fulfilling life.

And all it need take is *just sixty seconds a day*!

Acknowledgements

My grateful thanks to Cynthia Hemming for her valuable contributions in the production of this book; to Patricia Jowsey MFPhys ITEC for assistance with those techniques dealing with aromatherapy and massage; and to Sarah Hannigan, Victoria Hipps and Vicki Harris for their editorial work on the manuscript.

'The biggest problem in the world could have been solved easily when it was small.'

Lao-tzu

Contents

Guide to Techniques

How to Use This Book

I have divided *One-Minute Stress Management* into two parts.

Part One provides a general background to stress and explains how it is possible to manage many stress-related problems using procedures which can be learned and put into practice in one minute or less.

Because this book is intended as a practical guide to stress management, I have kept the technical explanations about the nature of stress to a minimum.

Part Two describes ways of measuring your stress, and provides more than forty practical procedures for managing stress, quickly and easily, under a wide variety of circumstances.

I suggest you begin by assessing levels of workplace stress by means of the questionnaire in Chapter 8. You may also find it useful to construct the stress barometer, as explained in Chapter 9, or to start to keep a stress diary, as suggested in Chapter 10.

These objective measures make it easier to decide which of those situations that you currently find stressful should be tackled first. Start by working with the procedures of greatest relevance to your current situation.

Because they can all be learned so easily you'll be able to put them to work for you right away. Continue with your selected procedure or procedures for a week to ten days, then review the situation.

You may also find it useful to repeat the assessment in Chapter 8 in order to see whether measurable benefits have resulted. You should also ask yourself:

Am I working more happily and enthusiastically?
Has my performance improved?
Do I feel more confident about tackling
    challenges that once proved stressful?
Do I feel more in control of events?
Have any symptoms of anxiety, such as a rapidly
    beating heart, dry mouth, churning stomach,
    and so on, decreased?

You should be able to answer 'yes' to most if not all of these questions. If so, continue using the procedures until they have developed into your natural response to these particular situations.

You can then learn additional procedures to help you manage any remaining stress in other areas of your life.

PART ONE

I

Sixty-Second What?

When I assure clients that they can control stress and use it creatively, in a minute or less, their first response is usually disbelief. Their second is irritation. They accuse me of taking their difficulties a great deal too lightly.

'I have a terrible boss, a shaky marriage, my teenage children don't understand me, commuting to work each day leaves me exhausted, my love life is non-existent, my debts are enormous and even my dog doesn't love me. How dare you tell me my stress problems can be solved in sixty seconds a day!'

By way of reply, I sometimes drop a lighted match on to some tissue paper placed in a metal ashtray on my desk. Because it's been dotted with alcohol, the paper flares up, then burns steadily.

Taking a glass from my desk, I pour a small amount of water over the flames, which are quenched immediately. 'A small fire can be brought under control quickly and easily,' I point out. 'But suppose those flames had been allowed to spread unchecked. In no time papers on the desk would start burning, then the desk, then the room. It would have taken hours to put out the flames. We'd have had to send for the fire brigade and tremendous damage would have been caused. The whole building might have been damaged beyond repair.'

I go on to explain that fire and stress have much in common. Uncontrolled, fire sweeps through forests or rampages through houses leaving death and devastation in its wake. Controlled, fire provides the energy to drive industry, heat our homes, power our cars, fly our jets and cook our food.

Similarly, uncontrolled stress is massively destructive to personal health and happiness; it wrecks careers, destroys relationships, undermines self-confidence and prevents you from achieving your true potential. Controlled stress, by contrast, is a potent source of creative energy which helps us live life to the full. To feel positive, creative and enthusiastic. To wake each morning inspired and energised by the prospect of fresh challenges to face and new goals to achieve.

Yet neither fire nor stress can easily be brought under control if allowed to rampage unchecked for too long.

Allow stress to get out of hand and it will eventually destroy you.

Catch stress early enough and you can transform it into a creative force for good in your life.

This book will tell you how.

Why Managing Stress Can be Stressful

There is a catch–22 with many widely taught stress-management techniques. They can leave you feeling even more stressed than before!

The problem is that most take weeks to master and need to be practised for fifteen to thirty minutes a day in order to produce any lasting benefit.

For hurrying high achievers, those usually described as having a 'Type-A personality', setting aside this amount of time in their already hectic schedules is both difficult and demanding. Even when they find the time, the techniques themselves can, at least during early sessions, increase stress.

These barriers to managing high levels of stress were first drawn to my attention by two clients. As with all the case histories used in this book, names and some details have been changed to protect confidentiality.

George, a World-Class Type-A

When we first met, George, aged forty-five, regularly worked an eighty-hour week in his job as managing director of a software company. During a typical seven-day working week he'd be juggling tight production schedules, worrying about cash-flow, and fighting for orders in an increasingly cut-throat market. On top of all this, George travelled constantly, visiting clients and suppliers in Europe, the US and Japan.

Aggressive, competitive and ambitious, George was

exactly the kind of individual that cardiologist Meyer Friedman MD, Director of the Recurrent Coronary Prevention Project in San Francisco, has identified as a Type-A. Only George was even more so. In fact, George was a world-class Type-A, for life just wasn't fast enough. He had turned impatience into an art-form. He hated any kind of delay. In restaurants, waiters served him on the double or risked a furious tirade. Even if he really wanted something, he'd storm out of a busy shop rather than wait to be served. Once, riding with him in an express lift, I watched as George tapped irritably at his watch. It was clear that even those few seconds of enforced idleness were unbearable to him.

Yet, despite the pressure, George loved his fast-track lifestyle and refused to accept that it could ever harm him. 'I don't suffer from stress,' he once boasted to me. 'I'm a carrier!'

But George was so wrong it almost killed him.

He was misled by a widely held belief that, if you really enjoy what you do, it can't be stressful. That, in some way, loving your job provides an antidote to crippling stress.

Unfortunately, this is like saying that if you adore eating and drinking, gluttony will never harm your health! A month before George consulted me, a routine medical check revealed him to be severely hypertensive, with dangerously high blood-pressure.

George was worried, and rightly. He knew that this level of hypertension significantly increased his risk of heart disease and kidney failure, while reducing life expectancy by up to twelve years.

So when his doctor suggested he learn Progressive Relaxation, George agreed immediately. This technique, which involves first tensing and then relaxing each of your major muscle groups in turn, was developed some fifty years ago by University of Chicago physiologist Edmund Jacobson. Studies have shown Progressive Relaxation lowers blood-pressure, reduces unnecessary muscle tension and creates a more tranquil state of mind.

8

The technique takes about three weeks to learn and requires regular sessions, each lasting about thirty minutes, to ensure results.

With some people Progressive Relaxation proves extremely beneficial. Unfortunately George was not one of them. In fact, it ended up making him even more stressed than before.

'My doctor gave me a tape cassette of instructions,' he recalls. 'I started working with it the moment I returned home.

'But after only a few minutes I found myself getting more and more tense and anxious. My mind started racing so fast that it was impossible to concentrate on the tape. The more I tried to unwind, the more tense I became. I called my doctor, and she said I must keep going. That it was natural to become more tense at first. But just lying there was sheer torture. After ten days, I found my blood-pressure had actually risen a couple of points. So I handed back the cassette and gave up any hope of controlling my stress through relaxation.'

Shortly afterwards, George consulted me and learned some of the one-minute stress-control techniques described in this book.

Today, without any major lifestyle changes, George's blood-pressure is normal. He no longer suffers from poor digestion or lower-back pain, and he enjoys more restful sleep. At work, both his problem-solving and decision-making skills have improved significantly. He is able to deal in a calm and effective manner with challenges that once sent his stress levels soaring.

George's difficulties are far from uncommon.

The more impatient and competitive people are, the more difficulty they will have in mastering Progressive Relaxation. Or, indeed, any technique involving lengthy training and regular practice, as is shown by my second case history.

Susan, a Two-Shift Career Woman

Like many career women, Susan, a thirty-three-year-old advertising executive and mother of twin daughters, worked two shifts: the first at work, the second when she returned home in the evening. From dawn to dusk her every activity had to be tightly scheduled. 'I used to joke that the only way I could allow myself to fall ill was if it had been timetabled in my appointment book,' she recalls.

Like George, Susan appeared to thrive on her demanding lifestyle. 'I kept fit, getting up at five o'clock every day, winter and summer, to go swimming. I played squash three times a week and took aerobics classes regularly,' she told me. 'I was so healthy, it never occurred to me I could fall victim to stress.'

Susan had been misled by a second widely held myth about stress: that being fit safeguards you against chronic stress.

In fact, your very fitness can make matters worse.

Because you appear so much better able to cope with a high workload than the less-fit people around you, there's a strong temptation on the part of bosses to dump all the most stressful challenges into your in-tray.

'I was always given the toughest assignments,' says Susan, 'because my boss believed I coped with them better than anyone else in the company. If there was an angry client to pacify, it was me they sent for. If there was a rush job to complete, I was always the first in line to be asked. I became the agency's troubleshooter, always in the middle of a commercial row.'

Because Susan was in such excellent physical health, she was able to work long and hard for years. Then, without warning, everything changed. 'I woke up one Monday morning and immediately suffered a panic attack. I'd never experienced anything like it before and felt terrified. My heart was thumping so fast I felt certain I was having a major heart attack. My husband called out our doctor, who could find nothing wrong. Tests confirmed that my heart was in great shape. The only problem was, I wasn't.

'From that morning on, for more than a year, each day was a nightmare. At work I found it hard to make the simplest decisions. My creativity nose-dived. I wasn't able to cope with tasks which, only a couple of weeks before, I'd have tackled with ease. My confidence was shot to pieces. Just getting up in the morning was a major effort.'

At her doctor's suggestion, Susan agreed to attend classes in Autogenics. Developed during the 1930s by Dr J. W. Schultz, a German neuropsychologist, Autogenic Training (AT) teaches people to relax by repeating such phrases as 'My hands and arms are heavy and warm. My breathing is deep and even.' As with Progressive Relaxation, Autogenic Training can be a powerful stress-management technique.

But for Susan AT proved anything but helpful.

'My problem was finding time to attend regular classes. It was a thirty-minute drive to the clinic and each session lasted around one hour. The only way I could fit this in was by giving up my squash and cutting down on swimming. Without this regular exercise I became increasingly tense. After I'd missed a couple of sessions because one of my daughters was ill, I gave up.'

I must emphasise that both Progressive Relaxation and Autogenic Training are excellent techniques which, when mastered, can prove powerful antidotes to stress. Indeed, later in the book I shall be describing a modified form of Progressive Relaxation.

But, in my professional experience, there is a substantial number of stress victims who are not helped by them. In fact, their stress levels are increased through attempting to master these demanding and time-consuming techniques.

And, having failed to obtain benefit from these highly recommended methods, they often despair of ever being able to control their stress.

At this point they may soldier on, grinning and bearing the stress until it finally lays them low with a serious mental or physical problem. They may self-medicate by taking powerful tranquillisers in the form of alcohol or potent stimulants in the form of nicotine. They may turn to even more damaging, and illegal, drugs. They may comfort-eat, so creating weight problems and risking loss of self-esteem. They may give up a career they love but can no longer cope with. They may take their stress problems out on their family, leading to a disintegration of relationships.

What they are not likely to do is seek out alternative, health-enhancing techniques of stress control.

Do You Respond Like George and Susan?

If, in my test at the beginning of this book, you under-estimated the passing of one minute by ten seconds or more, if you loathe queuing, are irritated by even minor delays when travelling and fume when caught in rush-hour traffic, it's likely that your response to some stress-management techniques will be the same as that of George and Susan.

Maybe you have already tried to master Progressive Relaxation, Autogenic Training, Yoga, Transcendental Meditation or some other stress-management techniques, without success.

If so, don't worry.

The techniques I describe in this book have worked for hundreds of sufferers.

As I have already explained, they are easy to learn and so quick to use that you can carry them out during any spare moments during the day:

> When commuting to work
> While waiting at a red traffic light
> In the few moments before rising to deliver a
>   speech

Immediately prior to a difficult meeting – or even
  during the meeting itself
During your mid-morning or afternoon breaks
When you are delayed at an airport, or during
  the flight itself

You can use them to unwind following some stressful challenge, to avoid carrying performance-harming tension into your next activity.

By spending sixty seconds destressing yourself at the end of a hectic day, you can avoid taking work-related stresses home with you.

Controlling stress this way does more than safeguard your health. It also enables you to carry out any task with maximum success and efficiency.

As I shall explain in Chapter 5, we can only achieve our true potential when our degree of mental and physical arousal is neither too high nor too low. A point which has been termed our 'Peak Performance Stress Level'.

But before we look at ways in which stress can be transformed into a creative force for good in our life, let's consider some of its more destructive consequences. Effects so damaging that they have led most people to equate stress with distress.

3

Stress and Your Health

A survey among financial institutions* revealed that sixty-four per cent of employers regard excessive stress as the principal health threat facing their company. Four times the number who cited heart disease, and six times as many as said alcoholism.

They are right to do so.

The same research suggested that around half of all absence from work in large companies can be blamed on stress-related illness.** It has been estimated to affect 1.4 per cent of the workforce at any one time, and to cause at least thirteen per cent of all sickness. In the United States, more than forty million working days are lost annually as a result of stress-related sickness. In the UK, where absenteeism on grounds of ill-health costs some £25 billion a year, forty per cent is attributed to stress.

Stress and Disease

When we become distressed, our adrenal glands, located above the kidneys, release adrenaline and noradrenaline into the bloodstream. These powerfully stimulating hormones, which are also produced by nerve cells, act as chemical messengers. Nerves releasing noradrenaline affect almost every organ in the body, including the eyes, intestines, bladder, tonsils and appendix.

People who have abnormally high levels of noradrena-

*Conducted by MORI on behalf of BUPA (1987).
**'The Mind Survey: Stress at Work' (1988).

line, caused by malfunctioning adrenal glands, have an above-average risk of coronary disease.

Some doctors believe that chronic stress has a similarly damaging effect on the heart. Dr Robert Karasek, of the University of Southern California, matched the incidence of past heart attacks in more than 4,800 men with the work they did. While the incidence of heart attacks in the entire sample was only 1.5 per cent, the rate among men with very stressful jobs was almost three times as high.*

In a study of resistance to illness, Dr Janice Kiecolt-Glaser and her colleagues from the Southern Methodist University of Dallas reported a decrease in the number of lymphocytes (white blood cells that are key defenders in the immune system) among medical students on the first day of their final exams. She also found that, during their exams, the students had diminished immune activity as well as a drastically reduced ability to produce the vital defence chemical *interferon*.

When experiencing excessive stress, not only is your body under direct attack from within, it is also far less able to defend itself from assaults from without. As your general health declines, mind and body become more vulnerable to further stress, so creating a vicious downward spiral.

One of the most destructive consequences of high-level chronic stress is 'Burn-Out Stress Syndrome', or BOSS, a 'psychological withdrawal from work in response to excessive stress'. BOSS's many ill-effects include:

Extreme reluctance to go to work each day
A profound sense of failure
Anger and resentment
Guilt, cynicism and self-blame
Intense fatigue, even on waking
Sleep and eating disorders

*Journal of Organisational Behaviour (1990).

Depression, a feeling of hopelessness
Loss of confidence and low self-esteem
Increased consumption of cigarettes, alcohol and
    drugs, prescribed and otherwise
An increase in minor health problems such as
    colds and flu, headaches, stomach upsets,
    back pain and missed menstrual periods

Once established, BOSS becomes a self-reinforcing process, as the negative attitudes and actions which result lead to further discouragement and withdrawal.

By controlling your stress you will also improve your health. By enhancing your health you improve your ability to combat stress.

But what creates that stress in the first instance?

4

Why You Suffer Too Much Stress

You will become stressed whenever the demands being made on you are greater than your capacity to cope. There are three ways this can happen.

1. Stresses affecting many people

Some stressors affect hundreds or even thousands of people at the same time, such as natural and man-made disasters: earthquakes, hurricanes, wars, riots, train or shipping accidents.

2. Stresses affecting smaller groups

A second type of stress is shared by smaller groups of people who are related to one another in some way, like factory workers threatened by redundancy or a family suffering bereavement. Major life-events – such as moving home, the end of an intimate relationship, serious illness of a loved one, children leaving home, being fired, retirement and, especially, bereavement – create significant increases in stress.

3. Stresses affecting individuals

Finally, there are the very personal stresses we endure as individuals, the majority of which are due to the hassles of life, such as commuting, aggressive clients, conflicts between career and family, working in noisy surroundings, and so on.

During the 1960s two American psychologists, Thomas Holmes and Richard Rahe, constructed a list of the most stressful events we can experience. These were then rated in terms of the amount of stress they imposed.

Event	Rating
Death of spouse	100
Divorce	73
Marital separation	65
Personal injury	53
Marriage	50
Being fired	47
Retirement	45
Sexual difficulties	39
High mortgage	31
Child leaving home	29

As you can see, although the loss of a loved one heads the list by a high margin, even events normally thought of as joyful, such as marriage, are also stressful.

The Nature of Workplace Stress

Research has shown that the most stressful organisations are those that combine highly competitive cultures with demands for total dedication. Today that means the vast majority of successful companies.

Asked to list the qualities needed for corporate success, ninety-three per cent of bosses made 'total commitment' their top qualification, while seventy-five per cent said a highly competitive nature was essential for climbing the corporate ladder.

But it's not only high-flying executive employment that creates excessive stress. According to a recent study, ten of the most stressful jobs are: inner-city teacher, police officer, miner, air-traffic controller, junior hospital doctor, stockbroker, journalist, customer-service/complaint-department worker, waitress and secretary.

Stress comes in many guises, as these brief extracts from my client files demonstrate:

> I have grown used to dealing with frantic deadlines, but this doesn't mean the stress gets any better. At the end of most weeks I feel absolutely drained.
>
> advertising copy writer, aged twenty-nine

> There is never enough time in the day to get done all that's expected of me. When I get home I'm exhausted, yet find it almost impossible to sleep. My health is suffering. I feel constantly tired out.
>
> financial consultant, aged fifty-two

> It sometimes seems I'm running flat-out just to stay one step ahead of the game.
>
> sales representative, aged twenty-six

Behind these very different descriptions of stress lies a single factor: a fear of losing control.

Dr Joseph Schwartz, a sociologist at the State University of New York at Stony Brook, believes that the amount of control a person can exert at work determines the amount of stress that job involves: 'How much freedom a worker has in deciding how to meet a boss's demands', he says, 'will determine if those demands actually produce stress.'

It is this independence – this freedom to regulate the significant events in one's life – that, I believe, lies at the very heart of effective stress control.

Stress and Control

Every major source of stress, from money worries to the threat of redundancy, from loss of a loved one to the ending of a relationship, from moving home to public speaking, has loss of control as its key element. The sense of helplessness which overwhelms us when nothing we do seems to make any difference to the outcome of events.

It's not that we don't usually struggle to retain control. But the ways chosen are either inappropriate or ineffective:

Parents stressed because they feel unable to control their teenage daughter, for instance, may continually lose their temper, causing the relationship to deteriorate even faster. A man who has lost his job through redundancy may seek comfort in drink.

The most widely used strategy for dealing with stress is avoidance. We close our minds and deny the reality of some stress-arousing situation: 'My job's as safe as houses,' insists the executive who has denied the reality of his imminent dismissal; 'We've got a wonderful relationship,' insist the couple whose marriage is on the verge of collapse.

Another popular technique is 'Undoing', the name Freud gave to the stress-reducing strategy of using ritual 'magic'. Wearing lucky charms, crossing your fingers, avoiding cracks on pavements are all examples of Undoing. The greater the stress, the more likely people are to resort to Undoing. There is nothing much wrong with believing in luck, provided you also take practical steps to overcome your stress-related difficulties. Used to excess, Undoing leads people to wait passively on events rather than taking active charge of their destiny.

The failure of these strategies increases stress by making us feeling even more helpless than before.

Whether or not you become over-stressed in any given situation, therefore, depends almost entirely on the degree of control you believe you can realistically exert over events.

Stress isn't out there. Stress arises from within. It stems from the interaction between what happens and your perception of what is happening.

By providing you with greater control over the effects of stress, the techniques described in this book will help to change your perception of challenging events.

In this way, even situations you now find intolerably stressful, and may have avoided, should become far easier to cope with – calmly, confidently and successfully.

5

How Stress Can be Good for You

Centuries ago, the word 'stress' described the amount and type of physical torture needed to extract a confession. In medieval dungeons, inquisitors used thumbscrews to crush limbs by exerting compression stress. Victims were stretched on the rack, which produced tensile stress. The spikes of the iron maiden sliced through flesh, applying what engineers term shear stress.

Today, although excessive workloads, financial worries, family disputes, urban congestion, deadlines and aggressive bosses have replaced the thumbscrew, rack and iron maiden, most of us continue to regard stress as a form of torture, something so deadly dangerous and distressing that it has to be avoided at almost any cost.

Stress Gets a Bad Press

Stress is associated with virtually every human misery and misfortune. It's become one of the buzzwords of modern life. You can't watch TV, listen to the radio or read a newspaper without being warned that stress either causes or is caused by something bad. Stress has been blamed for virtually every complaint of modern life, from premature ejaculation to absenteeism, from equipment breakdown to early death.

There's no doubt about it: stress gets a terrible press! This is not only unfair, but misleading.

This bad press has led millions of men and women to flee from stress as though it were an invading army, to abandon careers they enjoyed and which brought them great satisfaction for the supposed tranquillity of a rural lifestyle. Yet the truth is, we can never escape from stress, except at one particular moment in our lives: death.

The Life-Saving Stress of Being Born

Birth is probably the most stressful event we experience.

For several hours we are squeezed through the birth canal, sustaining severe pressure to the head, and being intermittently deprived of oxygen as placenta and umbilical cord are compressed by our mother's contractions. Suddenly we burst from the warm, life-sustaining protection of our mother's body into a harsh white, cold, oddly smelling hospital delivery room, where a giant holds us upside-down and slaps our buttocks.

No wonder that the brief journey from womb to world sends a baby's levels of adrenaline and noradrenaline soaring to a high not found even during a heart attack!

Yet without that stress we might not survive at all.

Far from being a terrible and dangerous ordeal, research shows that the stress of birth offers the best possible start in life.

The hormones prepare us for life beyond the womb by improving lung function, increasing the blood-flow to heart and brain, and stimulating the production of glucose to feed the brain and glycogen to feed the body. In addition, by making the newborn more alert, they help ensure that a close bond forms between mother and baby.

From the very first moments of independent life, therefore, stress proves essential and beneficial. If we learn how to control and use this potent force it will remain powerful and will continue to energise us throughout our lives.

The truth is this:

STRESS CAN BE GOOD FOR YOU

Hard as it may be to believe, this assertion is supported

by an increasing body of research evidence and personal experience.

During the mid-1950s Dr Hans Selye, the father of modern stress research,* distinguished between beneficial *eustress* (a word he coined from the Greek *eu*, meaning 'good', as in ('euphoric'), and performance-sapping *distress*.

More recently, studies by Dr Estelle Ramsey, a physiologist at Georgetown University Medical School, have shown that high achievers (men and women whose accomplishments have gained them a place in *Who's Who*) enjoy a longer and healthier life than the population as a whole. 'These are among the most driven people in the world,' Dr Ramsey comments, 'but, as a group, they're also among the healthiest.'

History shows us that many who have endured extremely stressful experiences are strengthened by their ordeal. Mahatma Gandhi, who led India to independence, spent more than 2,300 days behind bars and endured several lengthy fasts, yet remained sufficiently healthy and vigorous to become one of the twentieth century's most influential leaders.

How is this possible?

To understand how we can be stressed for success, imagine a violin string. Too slack and you can't play a note. Too taut and the string is in danger of snapping.

Only under exactly the right amount of stress will the string yield beautiful music. The same balance applies to stress.

This optimum point is our Peak Performance Stress Level (PPSL).

Peak Performance Stress

Several years ago, Russian sports psychologist Yuri Hanin suggested that athletic performance was linked to

The Stress of Life, McGraw-Hill, 1956.

24

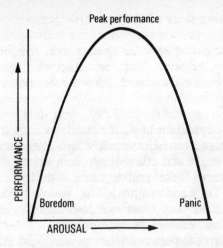

Peak performance

PERFORMANCE

Boredom   Panic

AROUSAL

The relationship between stress and performance
As you can see, up to a certain point increased stress
improves performance. But when we become
stressed beyond this critical level, our ability to
perform effectively declines with increasing
rapidity.

an optimal level of arousal. When under-aroused, you
feel bored, apathetic and lacking in competitive spirit.
Over-arousal, by contrast, leads to excessive anxiety,
confusion and a sapping of self-confidence. Today this
theory is widely accepted by psychologists, especially
those working with sportsmen and women.

What holds true on the playing field applies equally
to the factory floor, the office, the boardroom, and even
the bedroom!

If you are in management, major sources of stress will
include a high and often variable workload, responsibility for others, dealing with complex intellectual challenges and lengthy periods of intense concentration.
Your main problem will be *overstress*.

If you are in a blue-collar job, significant sources of
stress are likely to be insufficient job satisfaction, too

few opportunities to realise your true potential, lack of independence, routine unstimulating work, long hours, too little control over your destiny and, frequently, a noisy, dirty, dusty, hot or otherwise physically unfriendly work environment. Your main problem will be *understress*.

When you are at your PPSL you feel energetic, enthusiastic, confident and, above all, in complete control of events. You react quickly and effectively. You become a creative and efficient problem solver. Recall of facts and figures is fast and accurate. You feel alert and responsive. Your action time is fast, your control of fine muscles precise, your hand–eye co-ordination accurate. Your speed and endurance are optimum.

In short, you experience what psychologist Abraham Maslow dubbed a 'peak experience': one of those rare moments when everything seems to work perfectly, when you know for certain that your efforts will lead to success.

If your stress continues rising, however, your performance declines rapidly. You become increasingly uncertain, anxious, confused and unable to cope. Finally panic sets in.

Peak Performance Stress Varies Between Individuals

A situation that one person finds intolerably stressful may leave another feeling only pleasantly stimulated. Many journalists need adrenaline-pumping deadlines to write good stories. Some even delay getting down to the task, to increase the pressure and create a 'deadline high'.

By learning how to monitor your stress, and then adjust it either down or up according to the demands of a particular situation, you will be able to maintain a high level of performance.

At the same time you must be careful to safeguard yourself against unexpected increases in stress caused by events beyond your control. In order to do this it is necessary to keep your stress-bank balanced.

Keeping Your Stress-Bank Balanced

Using stress creatively can be likened to handling your finances prudently. As Charles Dickens's Mr Micawber put it: 'Annual income twenty pounds, annual expenditure nineteen nineteen six, result happiness. Annual income twenty pounds, annual expenditure twenty pounds ought and six, result misery.'

As with cash, so with stress.

Get Stressed – Pay the Price

To pay for stress, we draw on reserves of what I call our Stress Resistance Currency (SRC). Each time you get stressed, you pay out a sum in this currency. Unless you replenish your reserves you will get into stress debt. And that's when problems start.

Let's imagine that you start your working week with 100 units of Stress Resistance Currency. These have been built up during a relaxing weekend. Here's how you spend those reserves:

Over breakfast you have a pointless argument with your partner. This debits the SRC reserves by 15 units. The stress of driving to work through congested traffic debits a further 5 units from your account. You pay out 20 units dealing with the stresses of a normal working day. During the afternoon, a sudden office crisis sends your adrenaline surging and you rapidly spend 25 SRC units. Because you have been prudent in your spending you arrive home with 35 SRC units to spare.

27

Now let's picture a different scenario:

Over breakfast you argue with your partner. The cost of this row, as before, is 15 SRC units. Driving to work you get into a slanging match with another driver who is obstructing the road. This makes you late for the office and the exchange costs you a further 15 units. Arriving at work in a bad temper, you are irritable with a colleague, who snaps. That costs another 10 units. The daily pressures eat up a further 30 units because, being in a negative mood, everything seems that much more of an effort. A major crisis consumes 45 units. You arrive home so stressed and irritable that another row is inevitable. Sure enough, you get into a fight with your teenage son. The price: 20 units from the by-now-overdrawn SRC account. You have just gone into the red by 35 units.

And so it goes on, until the day arrives when a night's rest is no longer sufficient to replenish the SRC bank and you are overdrawn before getting out of bed.

At this point trouble starts.

In most of these situations spending your valuable Stress Resistance Currency did nothing to improve the situation and in most cases probably made matters worse.

You squandered finite reserves for no good reason. This doesn't mean that you should never stand up for yourself, argue, express an honest opinion or lose your temper. If that's what you feel like doing, go ahead. But bear in mind that there will be a price that must be paid.

The first rule of sixty-second stress control is simple. Consider each potentially stressful situation as a business transaction. Before drawing on your limited reserves, ask yourself if the return on investment is likely to be worthwhile.

Imagine that your Stress Resistance Currency is real money. Hard-earned savings.

Say to yourself: 'This is going to cost me X units of stress currency.' Place an arbitrary figure on the experience, depending on how stressful it's likely to prove.

Now ask yourself, just as you would before any

important purchase: 'Is it worth the price? Am I getting a fair return on my investment? Will this expenditure yield a benefit I cannot obtain in any other way?'

Reflect on possible alternatives. Can you negotiate a better deal? Could you achieve a similar result in a more cost-effective way?

Are you frustrated by slow traffic? You could rage at other motorists. Or you might decide to take a break and use one of the fast winding-down techniques described in the second part of this book before continuing with your journey. You might put on a tape of relaxing music, or distract yourself with a comedy programme on the radio.

Spend or save? Squander or conserve? The choice is always yours.

But bear in mind an old Spanish proverb: 'Take what you want from life, says God. And pay the price!'

By now the basic philosophy behind sixty-second stress management should be clear.

First, controlled stress is highly beneficial because it allows us to function, mentally and physically, at our peak of performance.

Next, in maintaining this peak level we spend out reserves of Stress Resistance Currency. To sustain an optimum level of stress we must always maintain a reserve of SRC. We can do this in two ways: by not squandering our reserves needlessly, in situations where becoming angry or upset will do not the slightest good; and by both replenishing diminished reserves and increasing these reserves using the techniques which I shall describe in Part Two.

In order to do any of these, we must first be able to monitor our levels of stress with a fair degree of accuracy.

The Importance of Monitoring Your Stress

A rule-of-thumb approach to deciding whether current stress is above or below your Peak Performance Level is to ask yourself: 'When tackling this task or dealing with this situation, do I feel confident and capable, excessively anxious, or largely apathetic over the outcome?'

If you welcome the challenge, enjoy what you are doing and perform to the best of your ability, your stress level is close to your PPSL.

When your performance fails due to anxiety or an inability to concentrate, chances are that the stress generated is too high.

If you couldn't care less about the task and are motivated mainly by the need for reward or fear of failure, your stress levels are probably too low.

Most of us recognise this, searching out stimulating activities if we get bored and trying to ease up, perhaps by taking time off, when the pressure gets too much. However, we may not always appreciate exactly how and why our stress has got out of balance. When overstressed, for example, it can be especially hard to pinpoint the precise nature of the problem sufficiently accurately to do much about it.

Alternatively, we may know perfectly well *why* we are feeling so stressed or so bored, yet feel trapped in the situation that is causing our difficulties.

On occasion, you may fail to notice just how rapidly stress is rising until your mental and physical health have deteriorated to a point where recovery is far harder and may require professional help from your GP or a clinical psychologist.

Stress levels are most likely to soar out of control in one of four circumstances:

1. When stress builds gradually

Imagine a half-filled glass of water. There is ample space to pour in additional fluid without any risk of overflow. Now picture the glass placed under a dripping tap. The level rises slowly but surely until the water is lapping at the rim. Once this point has been reached it only needs one more drop for the glass to overflow.

The same can happen with gradually building stress. If levels rise gradually, you may find yourself tipped over your Peak Performance Level by even a fairly minor additional stress.

This is what happened to Martin, an experienced and well-regarded lawyer. Normally easygoing and relaxed, twenty-six-year-old Martin suffered a series of relatively minor stresses over the course of two weeks. His wife, away nursing her widowed mother, had left him to look after their four-year-old twin boys. On the morning Martin's stress tumbler finally overflowed his babysitter arrived late, his car refused to start, there was a large and unexpected bill in the mail, he had cut himself shaving and his wife phoned to say she wouldn't be home that weekend as expected because her mother was still sick. Martin's normally well-ordered life was coming unravelled. His control was slipping. He reached his office with little capacity to absorb further stress and discovered that an appointment blunder had left him with thirty minutes to cross town for an important conference with a major client. Having reached his client's offices with only seconds to spare, Martin then discovered that important papers had been omitted from the file.

A calm and collected Martin would have simply phoned his secretary and told her to fax them over. But this incident was the final drop which caused his stress

glass to overflow. Angry and confused, he stopped thinking straight, tried bluffing his way through the conference and failed miserably. As a result, he almost lost a
top client, and he left the meeting embarrassed and
demoralised.

Had Martin known about the rapid stress-control techniques he was later to learn, that build-up of stress could
have been avoided. He would have known how to keep
the water in his glass at a level where there was little
risk of overflow.

2. When stress rises suddenly

If something goes unexpectedly wrong while you are
performing a task that is normally well within your
PPSL, an abrupt and catastrophic rise in stress may
occur.

One moment you are confident and in control. The
next panic has set in. This happened to Paula, an account
manager with a finance company, when her ten-year-old
son was knocked down by a car while crossing the street.
'One moment everything was fine and the next instant I
felt more stressed than I'd ever been in my life. Seeing
Mike lying there with blood on his face I could feel my
heart racing and my stomach churning. I couldn't think
straight or act sensibly. A policeman asked for my husband's work number so that he could call him. But I
just couldn't remember it. I only calmed down after we
reached hospital and I learned that, although Mike's leg
was broken, there were no more serious injuries.'

3. When stress is hidden

A third situation arises with activities that, although
creating high stress, are not seen by you as especially
stressful.

This applies particularly to tasks you greatly enjoy.
Here the pleasure that an activity provides conceals the
amount of stress involved.

Sid and his partner David worked hard for years building up one of the most successful car dealerships on the

south coast. 'Sid was a great strength with the customers,' David recalls. 'But occasionally something would go wrong and then he'd really blow his top. Looking back, we should have seen the signs of stress building in him, but business was roaring along so well, and we both enjoyed the challenges so much, that neither of us gave the stress of the job much thought.' Sid was especially worried by the prospect of letting customers down: 'If I said their car would be ready at four-thirty, then four-thirty it had to be,' he recalls. 'When I came home at night I'd bring my work with me. I'd be watching television but part of my mind would still be on the garage.'

One morning, following a row over a late delivery, Sid suffered a major heart attack. He survived but was unable to work again.

4. When stress is ignored

For many years the Third Avenue elevated railway ran through New York City. Then the line was closed down and the rails torn up. Not long afterwards, police began receiving early-morning phone calls from people living alongside the now abandoned track. They were complaining of strange sounds in the night, inexplicable odd noises that woke them from sleep. It was no coincidence that most of these calls were received around the time the first trains of the morning would have started running. Residents were being disturbed, not by the noise but by the unexpected silence! After years of living beside the track they had learned to ignore the noise of passing trains. But silence was new and strange.

Live with chronic stress long enough and, like passing trains, you stop noticing it, until the day dawns when your mind or body serves notice that something has gone badly wrong.

Carol, a middle-aged woman, found it very hard to deal with her domineering father-in-law. Because this caused her such stress she used the defence mechanism of 'denial' to cope. She refused to admit to anyone, herself included, that the confrontations were stressful. As a result she was unprepared to deal with the damaging effects of those soaring stress levels on her self-confidence and marriage.

Under these four conditions you may well find that your own stress rises out of control: beyond the point where quick and simple strategies will prove effective for restoring mind and body to normal function.

Whilst in a crisis there may be little or nothing you can do to prevent a sudden surge of stress – as in the case of Paula – there is still much that can be done to ensure your system returns to normal running as rapidly as possible.

When stress is increasing slowly and insidiously then vigilance and prompt prevention are essential. Listen to your body and act on any distress signals it is sending out. In addition to the symptoms of BOSS described on pp. 15–16, be on the look-out for these ten warning signs of rising stress:

> Irritability
> Fatigue, even after a full night's rest
> Impaired concentration
> Inability to perform as well as previously
> Sleeplessness, especially early waking
> Loss of enthusiasm and confidence
> Increasingly cynical outlook
> Aches and pains, in the head, jaw, neck,
>   shoulders and lower back
> Loss of appetite or a desire to binge on sugary
>   treats
> Low sex drive

In Part Two I shall describe fast, practical methods for managing the stress responsible for these and many other equally disagreeable and damaging symptoms.

PART TWO

8

Assessing Your Workplace Stress

This questionnaire allows you to compare your current levels of stress with the average for your occupation. Repeat it every few months or at any time when there are significant changes in your working situation.

Answer the following fifteen questions by choosing one of the responses given and scoring accordingly.

Response	Score
Does not apply	0
Never	1
Rarely	2
Sometimes	3
Rather often	4
Almost all the time	5

How frequently do you:
1. Find yourself without the authority to carry out all the responsibilities placed on you?
2. Have difficulty getting hold of the facts and figures needed to do your job efficiently?
3. Feel uncertain about the scope and responsibilities of your job?
4. Have such a heavy workload that it is impossible to complete all the tasks demanded of you during a normal working day?
5. Find yourself unable to satisfy the conflicting demands of the various people in your life?

6. Not really know what your supervisor or immediate superior thinks about you or how your performance is being evaluated?

7. Worry about the decisions you make that affect the lives of those working with you?

8. Fail to influence your superior's decisions or actions even though these affect you?

9. Find the demands of your job interfering with your personal and family life?

10. Find that your job requires you to do things against your better judgement?

11. Feel uncertain as to what is expected of you by your colleagues or superiors?

12. Find that the volume of your work makes it impossible to do the tasks as well as you would like?

13. Consider yourself insufficiently qualified to cope with the demands of your job?

14. Feel that you are not well-liked or accepted by those with whom you work?

15. Feel unclear about which opportunities for promotion or advancement exist within your job?

Add up your score.

Next, note how many questions were answered 'Does not apply'. Since these have no relevance you remove them from the final calculation by subtracting the number of zero-questions from the total number of questions asked. Suppose you gave six questions a zero score because they do not apply. Then you would have nine relevant questions.

Now divide your *total* score by the number of relevant questions and compare this figure with the average for your particular occupation in the Stress Chart below.

Two examples will help make the method clear.

Example 1 Suppose your total score is 59. Three of the fifteen questions received a zero score because they did not apply. This leaves twelve relevant questions. Your stress score is calculated by dividing 59 by 12, which gives 4.9. This indicates a high stress level for all occupations.

Example 2 Your score is 18 and you replied 'Does not apply' to two out of fifteen questions, so thirteen were relevant. Dividing 18 by 13 gives 1.4, a score indicating low stress for all occupations.

STRESS CHART

| Occupation | *Stress levels* | | |
	Low Stress	Moderate Stress	High Stress
Professional, technical	2.0	2.5	3.5+
Managerial	1.8	2.3	3.3+
Clerical, sales	1.8	2.3	3.3+
Craftsmen, foremen	1.7	2.2	3.2+
Semi-skilled/ unskilled	1.5	2.0	3.0+

Even if your stress score was on the high side, there is no need to worry. The procedures I shall describe will help you reduce your over-all stress level fairly swiftly.

If your score showed no current workplace stress problems, it would be sensible to repeat this assessment every few months to check that changing circumstances have not increased your stress.

9

Creating a Stress Barometer

While the quiz will help you gain a general overview of your stress levels, the following two methods are helpful in providing more precise early warnings of rising stress. You can use the stress barometer described below to confirm that you are neither rising above nor falling below your PPSL.

Constructing Your Barometer

Make your barometer when feeling confident, relaxed and close to your Peak Performance Stress Level.

Take two sheets of plain airmail-weight paper and place a sheet of carbon paper between them.

With a ballpoint pen, write half a dozen words across the centre of the paper. Apply the same amount of pressure as you would normally use when writing a letter to a friend. Beside this line write NORMAL.

Repeat the sentence at the top of the page, this time applying the lightest pressure required to produce a copy on the lower sheet of paper.

Write the sentence a third time at the bottom of the sheet, using the heaviest pressure possible without tearing the paper.

Repeat the sentence a fourth time, midway between your top (lightest pressure) and middle (normal) lines. Apply pressure halfway between your lightest and normal stroke. Beside this line, write RETREAT.

Finally, write the sentence between the middle (normal) and bottom (heaviest pressure) lines, applying

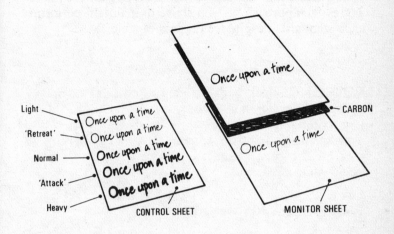

Light — Once upon a time
'Retreat' — Once upon a time
Normal — Once upon a time
'Attack' — Once upon a time
Heavy — Once upon a time

CONTROL SHEET

CARBON

Once upon a time

Once upon a time

MONITOR SHEET

a pressure midway between your normal and heaviest stroke. Beside this line, write the word ATTACK.

Now discard the top sheet and use the carbon copy as your barometer. Its greater contrast makes for easier use.

When you wish to monitor your changing levels of stress, take two sheets of paper with a carbon between them as before. Write the same sentence applying normal pressure.

Compare the most recent version with your original. If the pressure applied corresponds to your NORMAL line, your stress level is unlikely to have changed much. Where the handwriting pressure has become lighter, closer to the line on your barometer labelled RETREAT, your stress level is falling below the PPSL. You may be under-stressed.

If the line is heavier than your PPSL, if it more closely

matches the line labelled ATTACK on your barometer, your stress level is rising.

Decreased stress is more likely to produce a retreat from some challenging situations, because your motivation has declined. Increased stress suggests a more aggressive approach, as you strive to maintain performance standards despite feeling less capable.

Keeping a Stress Diary

To use stress creatively, you have to develop greater day-by-day awareness of especially stressful situations. This allows you to anticipate what I term our 'Red Buttons': those events and activities that automatically trigger a sharp increase in arousal. Only in this way can sudden surges in stress be prevented.

As well as identifying stressful situations, you must also become aware of how you felt, thought and reacted during these episodes. The most common method for doing this is to keep a stress diary. This can be done either in a pocket-size notebook or on index cards. Make the following headings:

STRESS DIARY – WEEK ONE

DAY: DATE: TIME:
SITUATION:
FEELINGS:
INTENSITY OF
FEELINGS:

The situation Be as precise as possible when recording these details, since you may find certain situations significantly increase stress. Include notes of: who else was present; what they were doing; what you were doing; when it happened; where it happened.

Time This is important because you may feel more or less stressed at some particular hour of the day, depending on such factors as your internal body clock – energy levels ebb and flow throughout the day – whether you are hungry and even the amount of daylight.

Feelings Include a brief note of your thoughts, emotions and bodily sensations, e.g. 'heart started beating more rapidly, mouth felt dry, light-headed etc.'.

Rate all these on a scale of 1–7, where 1 = Mildly stressful and 7 = Made me feel highly stressed.

A typical entry in your stress diary might read:

STRESS DIARY – WEEK ONE

DAY: Monday   DATE: 6 May   TIME: 10.25
SITUATION: In the office. Wondering how to cope with all the jobs that need to be done. Aware of noise of typewriters and phones from general office. My line manager tells me to complete a sales report by lunchtime. I try and explain that my already hectic schedule makes this impossible but objections are brushed aside.
FEELINGS: Anger and resentment, which I have to keep to myself. Fear of losing control over events.
INTENSITY OF FEELINGS: 6

Anticipation

The diary will help you to anticipate certain situations, which can then be mentally rehearsed prior to the event so as to reduce their subjective threat. Such rehearsals, carried out in a relaxed state, should be as detailed as possible. Try to hear and feel the scene being imagined instead of merely visualising it. Imagine yourself dealing with the challenge in a calm, confident and successful manner.

If keeping a diary seems too much trouble, another task to be fitted into an already hectic schedule, don't worry. There is a quicker way of recording stressful events, which takes no time at all and involves nothing more complicated than a length of string.

11

Keeping Stress on a String

If keeping a stress diary seems too much of a chore, here is a simple alternative.

Take a piece of string, around 8 ins (20 cm) long. Every time something stressful occurs, note it by tying a knot in your string.

Mark one end of the string in some way, such as with a drop of ink.

For stressful situations during the morning tie knots towards the uncoloured end of the string. For stresses later in the day tie a knot farther along the string.

If you experience a major stress, tie two or three knots in the same place.

For example, suppose you are delayed by morning-rush-hour traffic while driving to an important meeting. Your heart starts to race wildly as you worry about missing the appointment. You feel your hands sweating on the wheel. You silently curse the driver ahead, although you realise that losing your temper won't help. The next time your car slows to a halt, tie a knot at the beginning of your string.

At 11.30 a.m. you become involved in a dispute with a colleague and feel yourself getting tense. Tie a knot close to the middle of your string.

In the early afternoon, you call on an important client who keeps you waiting twenty minutes. As you sit in the reception area, your anger at the impolite treatment and worry over all the jobs still to be done back at the office cause your stress level to rise sharply. Tie two knots.

In the late afternoon a mountain of unexpected paper-work is dumped on to your desk. It's all urgent! Tie a knot towards the end of your string.

Just before going to bed, examine your stress string. Count the knots. Reflect on each. Bring to mind the stressful incident it commemorates as vividly as possible. Each knot will help you remember not only what happened, but how you responded to that situation: what you thought; what you said; the way your body responded; how you felt after the event.

Consider whether, during the period that your stress existed, you were above or below your Peak Performance Stress Level.

What could you have said differently – either out loud or silently – that would have reduced your stress or made it less painful? What might you have done differently?

Your answers will help guide you to the most appropriate technique for creatively using the stress involved in similar situations.

12

Testing for Negative Emotions

When I first describe this final method for assessing stress to clients, their reaction is often one of disbelief. I can well understand their scepticism since, on the face of it, the test appears highly improbable.

In fact, it not only works very well, but allows you to identify sources of stress operating below your level of conscious awareness.

All you do is this:

Stretch out your right arm (if right-handed) or left arm (if left-handed), and ask somebody to push downward while you resist their pressure.

Now bring to mind any person, situation, activity or challenge that might be creating excessive stress. If you do have negative feelings, your arm will be unable to resist the downward force, and start to descend. Where the emotion is positive, however, you will be able to continue resisting their pressure.

In this way it becomes possible to monitor your reactions to *any* potentially stressful action, even though you were not previously aware it was causing, or likely to cause, difficulties.

And, by focusing your mind on a positive idea, you will strengthen your arm's resistance to the downward pressure.

Naturally you can only test two or three different thoughts in the same session, or normal muscle fatigue will cause the arm to droop. But, after a few moments to recover, the test can be repeated.

Why should this work?

It is important to understand that, just as every sound, sight, taste, smell and touch produces a physical effect on the body, so too do thoughts, whether these are positive or negative, constructive or destructive.

If you experience an intensely negative emotion, for even a short amount of time, your mind and body become fatigued. Unhappiness also depletes reserves of energy, which is why being depressed is such an exhausting emotion.

Even pretending to experience an emotion is stressful. Research has shown that merely wearing a sad expression speeds up the heart-rate. A soothing image, such as a peaceful country scene, lowers blood-pressure and produces brain activity with a relaxed mental state.

All this happens within a few hundredths of a second, and normally without our even being aware of what is happening.

You can test the subtle interaction between mind and body, thought and action, by the following simple experiment. Draw a circle on a sheet of plain paper. Now construct a small pendulum by attaching a weight to a piece of thread about 8 ins long. The weight should be heavy enough to keep the thread taut and allow it to swing easily in any direction. Hold your hand steady above the circle, with the tip of your pendulum over the centre.

Concentrate hard on the idea that the pendulum will start swinging in a clockwise direction. Focus on this thought strongly, but keep your hand as steady as possible.

After a few moments, despite the fact that your hand appears not to have moved even a fraction of an inch, the pendulum will start moving clockwise around the circle. Once started, it will gradually pick up speed until the initial, fairly tentative movement has become a clear and unmistakable oscillation.

Now focus on the thought that the pendulum should move anticlockwise. Sure enough, it will hesitate, oscillate uncertainly for a while, then start moving in the required direction.

There is nothing mystical or magical about any of this, although some people may try to persuade you that there is. All that is happening is that your concentrated thought is being transformed into muscle movements so slight and subtle as to be imperceptible to the naked eye. But, when amplified by the length of the thread, they are sufficient to produce the desired movement.

The message is clear:

Unproductive thoughts always cause you harm, even if nobody else is aware of them.

Destructive ideas do not have to be translated into action to do damage. The negative thinker always suffers. Silently snarl, 'I hate you,' or 'I'd like to kill you,' and it's your own system that becomes the first victim of that mental poison.

Positive ideas exert exactly the opposite effect. They lower stress, strengthen the immune system and stimulate mental and physical well-being.

13

Changing Your Mind About Stress

The fastest way to reduce stress is to change your mind about a currently stressful situation. As the Roman author Epictetus remarked in AD 60: 'Man is disturbed not by things but by the views he takes of them.' Shakespeare echoed these sentiments by having Hamlet say: 'There is nothing either good or bad, but thinking makes it so.'

Philosophers and psychologists down the ages are agreed that it is often our perception of events, rather than the events themselves, that causes excessive stress.

The Stress that Impoverished Nicky

When thirty-three-year-old Nicky was fired from a brokerage house her stress levels soared and stayed chronically high. 'I felt so deeply ashamed, I cut myself off from all my old friends,' she told me. 'I wallowed in depression and self-pity, constantly reminding myself what a failure I was.'

As a result of this pessimistic outlook, Nicky's self-esteem nose-dived and she quickly came to see herself as a born loser.

After being unemployed for only three months, Nicky accepted a job with lower status, a lower salary and fewer prospects than her previous job, largely because she had convinced herself that she was unworthy of anything better.

The Stress that Enriched John

Contrast this response with that of John, aged thirty-two, after he lost his job at the investment bank where he had worked for ten years.

'At first I was devastated. The whole ritual of clearing my desk into a plastic bag and being escorted from the premises by Security was horrible. I felt deeply ashamed and humiliated.

'But the black mood lasted only a few days. Then I managed to view my situation in a more positive light, to see what had happened as an opportunity instead of as a threat to my future success.'

Because of this positive attitude, John's stress quickly returned to his PPSL. Calmly and optimistically, he reviewed all his options and developed a realistic plan to recover control over events. 'I decided to become an independent financial consultant. Although the going was tough, I never lost faith in myself.'

Within twelve months John had built a considerable reputation and a list of blue-chip clients, including the very bank which had fired him the previous year.

Two similar situations which provoked very different responses. For John, the stress of being fired became a spur to make positive changes in his life. For Nicky, excessive stress, fuelled by self-blame and negative thinking, swiftly spiralled into chronic distress, with catastrophic consequences.

The main difference between those who can change their minds about a stressful event and those trapped into a cycle of increasing distress lies in how optimistic or pessimistic they are.

Optimism, Pessimism and Stress

Because a pessimistic attitude is stressful, looking on the dark side will undermine your mental and physical health.

Optimism, in contrast, promotes your well-being and is life-enhancing.

In one study, a hundred healthy young men were divided into pessimists and optimists on the basis of their answers to a questionnaire. Their medical condition was then monitored over the next two decades.

By the age of forty-five, a majority of pessimists were displaying signs of chronic diseases, including heart attacks and arthritis. The optimists suffered far fewer of these health problems at forty-five, and remained in better general health into their later years.

An optimistic outlook may even help restore you to health following a major illness.

During the late 1980s, Professor Martin Seligman of the University of Pennsylvania and his colleagues studied video-taped interviews made eight years earlier by 122 men who had suffered their first heart attack. These were divided into pessimists and optimists on the basis of their answers during that interview. Out of the sixteen most pessimistic men, fifteen were dead; but of the sixteen most optimistic, only five had died.

The Role of Positive Pessimism

These findings do not mean pessimism has no role to play in life. When used appropriately, pessimism can actually help you to reduce stress and avoid what could prove costly mistakes, since pessimists are often able to confront reality more clearly and directly than optimists.

When the price of failure could be substantial, such as deciding whether to say or do something that might destroy a valued relationship, it is a good strategy to switch into pessimistic thinking to consider the worst possible outcomes.

How We Explain Our Successes and Failures

Martin Seligman has coined the phrase 'learned optimism' to describe how some people explain what happens to them in life. Pessimists blame bad things, such as marriage difficulties or job loss, on problems which are pervasive, enduring and their own fault. Optimists view the causes of failure as limited to that specific situation, short-term, and due to circumstances beyond their control. These differences are crucial in determining how much stress you will suffer.

Mark, aged twenty-nine, placed a very pessimistic interpretation on his failure to impress a promotions board. 'Just another disappointment in a lifetime of failure,' was his gloomy conclusion. 'I'll never succeed because I lack the talent to get ahead.' This explanation was *pervasive* ('another disappointment'), *enduring* ('I'll never succeed') and *self-blaming* ('I lack the talent').

Mary, a self-assured twenty-seven-year-old, came up with an entirely different explanation for her poor showing at a job interview at which she arrived late because her car broke down. 'I made a mess of things this time, but it won't happen again,' she said confidently. 'I've learned important lessons which will ensure that I do better next time.'

Her explanation was *limited* to that specific event ('I made a mess this time'), *short-term* ('it won't happen again') and *caused by events beyond her direct control*. Finally, she regarded her poor performance as a *learning experience*, which would help her do better the next time.

Pessimism and Irrational Thinking

When things go wrong, if you offer yourself explanations that involve more than this specific situation, blame yourself and regard each failure as part of a continuing saga of setbacks, your outlook is over-pessimistic and your stress levels are likely to remain high.

When something goes right, you'll probably switch explanations. Now your success is seen as due to *external causes* ('I got lucky for once') and only *temporary* ('it won't happen again').

After he'd passed a business examination with higher

than expected grades, Tony, aged twenty-nine, told me: 'It was sheer luck [external cause]. The paper was so easy [specific to that one exam]. There's no way I can ever be so lucky again [temporary state of affairs unlikely to be repeated].'

Pessimism, a major source of excessive stress, arises from irrational thinking. The ten most common of forms of irrational thought are:

1. All-or-nothing thinking
You tell yourself, 'Either I succeed at everything I attempt or I will be a total failure.'

Remember, the only way to learn is by making mistakes. In fact, if a job's worth doing, it's worth doing badly! The only way we ever get anywhere in life is by building on the foundations of past errors. That's how as a child you learned the most basic lessons of walking, talking and making sense of the world.

'Labelling' is an extreme form of all-or-nothing thinking. Here, as a result of a few mistakes, or even a single error, you constantly label yourself: 'I am worthless.'

2. Filtered thinking
Involves focusing on mistakes while either ignoring successes entirely or insisting that they 'don't count'.

3. Over-generalised thinking
You look on a single event as part of a pattern of inadequacy: 'Because this relationship has failed, it must mean that I am incapable of ever sustaining an intimate relationship with anybody.'

4. Mind-reading thinking
You assume that somebody thinks badly of you, without any evidence to support such a belief.

5. Fortune-telling thinking
You predict that things will turn out badly before even attempting a challenge.

6. *Magnification thinking*

You exaggerate your problems and shortcomings.

The opposite is 'minification thinking'. You greatly diminish or dismiss the value of benefits and rewards as insignificant. This is sometimes called 'binocular' thinking, since events look either larger or smaller than they actually are, depending on which end of the glasses is used.

7. *Emotional thinking*

Insisting that your negative outlook provides an objective view of how things really are. For example: 'Because I feel guilty about what has happened I must be a bad person.'

8. *'Should' thinking*

You believe that things should always be the way you hoped or expected them to be, telling yourself, 'I should feel this way,' or, 'I should expect this to happen.'

9. *Self-blaming thinking*

Holding yourself personally responsible for events that are not under your control.

10. *Social expectations thinking*

You assume that people must behave towards you in a certain way if you are to enjoy self-respect. Common examples are: 'I expect others always to . . . treat me fairly/keep their promises/look on me as special/reward my hard work/tell me the truth/recognise and appreciate my talents/show me gratitude when I am kind to them/ love me as much as I love them.'

Because all these are absolutes, they generate far greater stress than such realistic expectations as: 'It would be nice if people always treated me fairly, but I can't expect this will happen any more than they can assume that *I* shall always treat *them* fairly.'

To control stress and ensure that fresh challenges are

tackled with a positive attitude, change your mind about the way you view inevitable setbacks, mistakes and disappointments.

Check whether your ideas on a particular subject fall into any of the ten irrational-thinking traps described above.

Ask yourself whether you are attributing a lack of success to *internal*, *general* and *enduring* causes. Try to see them as being equally due to events which are, at least to some extent, *external*, *specific* and *limited*.

Do not become a victim of your own biography. A history of past setbacks need not predict future failures, unless you allow it to do so. Keep in mind the story of Thomas Edison, who tried a thousand ways of making a light bulb, without success, before finally hitting on the right method. When somebody suggested he had failed on a thousand occasions, the inventor replied: 'On the contrary, I have discovered a thousand ways by which you *cannot* make a light bulb.'

Remember too a comment made by the great Irish playwright George Bernard Shaw: 'As a young man,' he said, 'I soon realised that nine out of ten things which I attempted would fail. I therefore resolved to do ten times as many things.'

Review every situation as objectively as possible, preferably when you feel rested and relaxed. Step back from the situation and, without being unrealistic, seek out explanations that are rational and optimistic.

14

Coping With the Stress of Change

As the pioneering work of Thomas Holmes and Richard Rahe showed (Chapter 4), major life-events, such as moving home, ending an important relationship, redundancy or retirement, are highly stressful.

Here are some practical suggestions for bringing these often extremely high levels of stress back under control.

1. Show your emotions

Never feel embarrassed about being emotional. Expressing your feelings openly acts as a safety valve.

Chemical analysis of the tears shed by people experiencing a strong emotion shows that these are significantly different from tears produced physically by, for example, peeling onions. This difference leads some psychologists to believe that crying removes stressful chemicals and restores the body's chemical balance. It is undoubtedly true that a good cry helps you feel better. In one study, eighty-five per cent of women and seventy-five per cent of men said crying had a positive effect on their mood.

In another study, a group of healthy men and women were compared with others, of similar age and background, suffering from stress-related disorders. The main difference found between these two groups was that the stress sufferers considered weeping a sign of weakness, struggled to remain dry-eyed and felt ashamed if they did cry. The healthy people saw crying as natural and normal. They felt no embarrassment over shedding tears.

Other studies have found that widows who weep after

their husbands die are less likely to suffer stress-related illness than those unable or unwilling to grieve openly.

2. *Understand that time will heal*

It is normal – and essential – to pass through recognised stages of grieving whenever you have experienced a major loss.

The first stage is denial. An instinctive reaction to bad news is to gasp, 'No, no!'

The second stage is guilt, as you reproach yourself with such thoughts as: 'If only I had behaved differently, this might never have happened!'

Following closely comes anger, directed towards the other person: 'How could he cause me such pain?'

Do not repress these feelings. They are a natural part of the grieving process. They must be worked through before you can come to terms with your loss. Always allow yourself to mourn.

Once the first shock has passed, however, it is essential to stop brooding about what might have been and to start searching for any good features in the change. Whilst these may be very hard to identify, there is usually at least a glimmer of hope in even the most tragic of circumstances.

Review any new opportunities that have been opened up by the change. Seek to replace what has been lost with new activities that are pleasurable and rewarding. For example, a new widow or widower might spend more time with grandchildren and take pleasure from telling them stories or teaching them new skills.

3. *Talk to friends*

Numerous studies have confirmed that support and comfort from family and friends are powerful antidotes to excessive stress.

One study, by Dr Win Bolton at the University of Sussex, for example, found that the single most important factor in preventing depression among men who had been unemployed for more than six months was a network of supportive friends. The more close friends you have, the happier you will feel and the longer you are likely to live. You run less risk of becoming depressed, and will recover faster, all other things being equal, from surgery or a heart attack.

So talk about your problems, fears and feelings. Be willing to confide in those closest to you.

4. *Value your independence*

Once this crisis is over, take prompt action to reduce excessive dependency on friends or family and reassert responsibility for your own life. Only in this way can you regain control over events and rebuild lost confidence and self-esteem.

5. *Anticipate change*

While some changes happen so unexpectedly that no anticipation and planning are possible, many can be predicted in advance:

Children grow up and leave home. Plan to cope with the difference that this will make to your life.

You will, at some stage, retire. Instead of allowing retirement to creep up on you almost unawares, prepare for the many changes this will bring about.

With any predictable change, start anticipating as early as possible, because time has a habit of slipping past with remarkable speed.

6. *Create a life-plan*

Anticipation and preparation are far easier if you have an over-all plan for your life.

The starting point for creating such a plan is to establish goals, those things you intend to accomplish in terms of your family, social life, career and leisure pursuits. An effective if somewhat macabre method for deciding on life goals is to prepare your own ideal obituary!

You can do this by completing the form below. Don't respond as if your life were going to end tomorrow, but when, where and how you would ideally wish it to draw to a close. Write down, not your present accomplishments, however considerable, but ambitions waiting to be fulfilled.

_____ died in _____
your name   *where you would like to live*

_____ worked as a _____
your name   *career you'd most enjoy*

achieving the position of _____
                                        how high you hope to rise

Away from work_____'s chief interests

were _____

_____
hobbies, leisure activities, interests

_____'s many achievements included

_____
what you already have or aim to have accomplished

_____ will be remembered for _____
                                        what you wish to achieve

This fantasy obituary will help you identify your major goals in life. Having done that, it is easier to work out the practical steps which must be taken if your goals are to be achieved.

Here's an example of such a fantasy obituary:

Peter died last night in his luxury villa on a romantic Pacific island. Peter worked as a company executive, achieving the position of chairman. Away from work, <u>Peter's chief interests were his wife and children, with whom he had a warm relationship</u>. His hobbies <u>included diving, sailing and swimming</u>. Peter's many achievements included <u>giving generously to charity and helping to support many worthwhile causes</u>. He will be best remembered for <u>his friendship, generosity and good company</u>.

Having written your obituary, ask yourself what you are doing to turn those dreams into reality.

'Peter' decided to take more active steps to safeguard his health by being careful about his diet, getting more exercise and becoming less hostile. He studied to acquire new management skills, spent more time with his family and joined a diving club.

Ask yourself: 'Where would I like to live and what do I hope to have achieved – in the next twelve months [short-term goals]; in the next two to five years [medium-term goals]; five or more years from now [long-term goals]?'

Establishing goals and preparing a plan, which anticipates and prepares for inevitable change, enables you to avoid unnecessary stress.

A therapist friend once remarked to me that while some of us have more alligators to wrestle with than others, and while some of us are better at alligator-wrestling, there comes a time in everybody's life when even the best wrestlers are at risk of being eaten alive! She was referring to events so highly stressful that, if only in the short term, we are overwhelmed.

Even in these extreme circumstances, however, it is possible to avoid being eaten alive by stress, provided you anticipate, plan, and use the strategies described above.

15

Coping With the Stress of Time

How often do you feel excessively stressed by any of these situations:

Having too little time during the day to finish all your work projects

The feeling that time is passing far too rapidly and without you achieving your key goals in life

Not spending enough time with your family or friends

The speed with which time seems to be passing

If you find yourself sharing some or all of those difficulties, you could be in need of more effective time management.

What Goes Wrong

Philip G. Zimbardo of Stanford University speculates that the way we use time reveals something about our mental and physical health. In a study with Dr Alexander Gonzalez, Chairman of the Psychology Department at California State University, Zimbardo identified a number of different 'Time Zones' into which people can become fixed. In relation to stress the most significant Zones are:

Zone One – Present-Fatalistic There is little or no sense of urgency. Even when things don't get done on time, people in this Zone are seldom concerned. They often move and talk slowly, dislike deadlines and find it hard to be punctual. They suffer little or no time-related stress.

Zone Two – Present-Hedonistic People in this Zone are impulsive, dislike planning, make decisions on the spur of the moment. These people suffer mild stress by being constantly on the go.

Zone Three – Future-Oriented People in this Zone are constantly looking to the future rather than living in the present. They buy life insurance, try and plan everything well in advance and take deadlines very seriously. They experience moderate time-related stress.

Zone Four – Time Press This Zone is largely inhabited by Type-A personalities like George, my workaholic client whom we met in Chapter 2. People in this Zone set challenging deadlines and are preoccupied with getting things done on time. Unsurprisingly, they are the most affected by time stress.

Which Zone do You Occupy?

The test at the start of this book, where I asked you to judge the passing of sixty seconds, helps to identify whether time stress is a problem for you.

Repeat that test now, using the more detailed analysis below:

Glance at your watch then close your eyes.

Sit still until you judge that sixty seconds have passed.

Open your eyes and check.

Time elapsed, thirty seconds or less You are likely to be in the Time Press Zone and find this source of stress a significant problem.

Time elapsed, thirty to fifty seconds You are under a fair amount of time stress and may have difficulty satisfying conflicting demands for your time.

Time elapsed, fifty-one to sixty-plus seconds Your approach to life is sufficiently relaxed to make it unlikely that time stress is much of a problem.

63

The secret of coping with a hectic schedule is to allow yourself recovery periods between bouts of high activity. These need not be lengthy. A recuperation period lasting no more than one minute can restore you to your Peak Performance Stress Level.

Later in this book you will find ways to recoup your energy by using special breathing, relaxation and massage techniques.

Stress and Time Management

While efficient time management will help you to find a few more hours in a week, it will not reduce your stress by any significant amount. That newly found time will be filled instantly with other tasks, some of which may be more stressful than those you have just discarded.

Suppose you decide to stop reading junk mail to make time for preparing an extra report per week. Spending a few moments each day idly glancing through brochures and mail-order offers might have been quite relaxing, whereas producing another report might be rather stressful.

Therefore, although I will provide some ideas for using time efficiently, the most effective way of coping with time stress is to change your perception of time itself.

What to do

Step 1: Making more time for yourself
Start by setting major goals in the key areas of Family, Social, Career and Leisure. It then becomes possible to assign priorities to various activities, according to their relevance in enabling you achieve those goals. As a result you will find it far easier to respond appropriately to various demands on your time.

When faced with any task you have only four options. You can Drop it, Delay it, Delegate it or Do it.

Drop it This sounds easy, but breaking established

patterns requires determination and self-discipline. Check for time-wasting habits in your routine. Before carrying out any activity, ask yourself: 'Will this help me achieve a goal in life?' If the answer is no, then there is little point in investing even a few minutes of your life in carrying it out.

Delay it Negative delay or procrastination involves replacing a high-priority activity with one of much lower priority. You know you should be preparing a difficult report, but instead you squander time on the very low-priority task of tidying your desk. This avoidance strategy only increases stress later.

Positive delay is involved when:

> You postpone a low-priority task for one with a high priority
>
> You put off a task that arouses powerful and disruptive emotions, such as anger, fear or jealousy
>
> You have insufficient information or lack the requisite amount of skill to undertake the task efficiently
>
> Your physical or mental state is such that it seems unlikely you could carry out the job successfully

Delegate it Effective delegation is one of the greatest time-stress savers there is. Not only does effective delegation enable you to assign more time to tasks that only *you* can perform, it usually means a better job is done by everyone.

Do it This is the stage where many people fail. Although they have clearly identified a high-priority job, they can never find the right moment to begin.

As a final chore, spend a minute each evening mentally going over your schedule for the following day. Set aside time for routine tasks and those you simply can't avoid. If possible, begin with the more demanding tasks and leave the easier ones until later in the day. That way you'll be investing your energy more efficiently. Your plan must be sufficiently flexible to cope with the unexpected: the unscheduled meeting, an unexpected visit from a major client, the surprise party invitation, that last-minute panic to meet a sudden rush deadline, and so on.

This is where setting yourself clearly defined goals proves especially helpful. Since you are obliged to handle the unexpected or to cope in an emergency, it becomes far easier to decide which of your other commitments can best be dropped, delayed or delegated.

To test whether your time will be well spent, ask whether a proposed task is:

Necessary – not just enjoyable but essential? *Appropriate* – something you should be delegating? *Being done efficiently* – is there a better, faster, more time-effective way of doing it?

Step 2: Learn to switch your Time Zones

Identify Time Zones that you inhabit most frequently from the test at the start of this chapter and practise moving between them.

If, for instance, you prefer to plan well ahead, a characteristic of Zone Three, move into Zone Two occasionally by adopting some of the following strategies:

> Do something you have never done before, on impulse. Don't try to make any plans. Just do it
>
> Take off your watch and live the day according to how you feel. Eat when you are hungry rather than at a set time
>
> Get into the car and head off in any direction that takes your fancy. Drive for an hour without any objective in mind other than that of travelling
>
> Instead of planning a short-break, call into the travel agent the day before you are due to travel and take whatever is on offer

Go to the cinema and see a film without bothering
to read any of the notices first

On your next day off, decide what you want to
do when you wake, not the night before

Change your routine. Wear different clothes,
shop at unfamiliar shops, try eating food
you've never tasted before

Similarly, if you favour a high-pressure, Zone Four
approach to life, try moving into a Zone One frame of
mind now and then by allowing yourself to be more
relaxed about deadlines. This is especially important for
Type-As, who deliberately put themselves under time
pressures. Here are some suggestions:

When making appointments, say, 'I'll be with
you around nine-thirty tomorrow' instead of
specifying, 'I'll see you *at* nine-thirty.'

Take up a hobby that cannot be hurried, such as
painting, pottery, model-making or
gardening

Learn how to juggle. This can be a great way for
time-pressured people to wind down

Set your alarm fifteen minutes earlier than usual
and spend that time just lying in bed instead
of leaping up the moment the bell rings

Go on a journey lasting at least sixty minutes, by
train, plane or bus, without taking anything
to read or any work to do. Spend the time
studying the view from the windows or
observing your fellow-travellers

Deliberately leave unimportant work undone
until you stop feeling guilty

Step 3: Create a time stretcher
When you are physically and mentally relaxed (See
Chapter 23), visualise some place that is special to you.
Spend sixty seconds there, silently repeating, 'All time

is now. I have all the time I need for productive dreams.'
After a minute, open your eyes. You'll feel not only
more relaxed but also refreshed by the change of pace.

Step 4: Slow time with a yo-yo

Buy a yo-yo in a bright, cheerful colour. Find one
that moves smoothly. Whenever you feel time stress
building up, play calmly with your yo-yo for sixty
seconds. Focus on the movement of the yo-yo and practise making it rise and fall as slowly as possible.

Winding down with a yo-yo helps for three reasons.
First, it causes you to concentrate on something outside
yourself, so providing a distraction from stress. Second,
the rhythmic action is soothing and may assist the logical
left and intuitive right sides of the brain to integrate
more efficiently. Finally, the childlike aspect of 'playing'
with a toy is comforting and reassuring at periods of
great stress. It liberates you from the constraints of the
adult world, re-creating a period of your life when it was
possible to forget everything by going out to play.

16

Coping With the Stress of Failure

We are all guilty of talking ourselves down from time to time: undermining our self-confidence and threatening our self-esteem by embarking on internal conversations which focus solely on our mistakes. By doing so, we significantly increase stress, squandering precious SRC to no good effect. These unhelpful dialogues are most likely to occur whenever you:

> Fail to achieve an important goal
> Do not perform as well as expected
> Are rejected by someone you love
> Make a silly error or unwise decision
> Fail to satisfy the expectations of others

What to do

At random times during the day, pause and ask: 'What am I saying about myself at this moment?'

Regular monitoring is important because it's all too easy to slip into a habit of thinking negatively. Your automatic response to a setback can become 'I'll never cope with this,' 'How could I be so stupid?', and so on.

There are two occasions on which the stress created by silent self-criticism is especially harmful:

> Immediately before a significant challenge
> Immediately following an unexpected setback

At such times it is especially important to reflect on

what is about to happen, or has just occurred, as object-ively as possible. The best way of doing so is to step outside yourself.

Imagine seeing events through the eyes of a trusted friend or colleague. Consider how the situation must appear to them. Ask yourself: 'What advice would he/she be most likely to give me under these circum-stances?'

Consider whether you have fallen into any of the irrational-thinking traps described in Chapter 13. If so, find a more realistic explanation for what has happened. One of my clients found he was far more likely to make mistakes in the morning than during the afternoon. He was one of those people whose natural biological rhythms mean they are more alert later rather than earlier in the day. Having recognised this pattern, he switched his routine tasks to the morning and saved major decisions for after lunch.

When unfairly criticised by others, we are usually quick to defend ourselves. But if the criticism comes from within, accusations are more likely to stay unchal-lenged.

If somebody said, 'You are stupid,' you'd probably refute their charge with vehemence and offer examples of the many occasions on which you have behaved in a highly intelligent manner. Yet if you tell yourself, 'I am stupid,' you are more likely passively to accept that damaging and unfair judgement.

Whenever you detect a negative thought or statement, counter it at once with a more realistic comment. For example, following a mistake you silently tell yourself: 'What a stupid person I am.' From now on, respond with a spirited, 'I made a mistake. But most of the time I enjoy success. So let me reflect carefully on what happened to see what I did right, as well as wrong.'

Making this positive analysis your immediate response to blunders prevents you brooding on the setback. It also encourages you to challenge all unhelpful comments from others as they arise. Get into the habit of finding a realistic but optimistic explanation for failures. Doing so sustains your motivation and enthusiasm, ensuring stress remains at Peak Performance Level.

17

Coping With the Stress of Criticism

There is a well-known business adage which runs: There are two types of criticism. *Destructive* criticism is where the boss says you are an idiot; *constructive* criticism is where the boss explains precisely *why* you are an idiot!

Unfortunately, a large number of employers seem to believe that these are the only ways of criticising. As a result, they send stress levels soaring, usually without correcting the mistakes their criticisms were intended to cure.

Some people are far more stressed by criticism than others. The first step is to decide whether you are one of them.

How do You Respond to Criticism?

Score statements: 1 = Not true at all; 2 = True to some extent; 3 = Entirely true.

> I become upset when criticised.
> I lack confidence.
> I depend on others.
> I dislike new challenges.
> I seek frequent reassurance.
> I need the approval of superiors.
> I feel very upset by failure.
> I am unsure of myself in unfamiliar situations.

Score 19–24 You are extremely stressed by all types of criticism, even when such remarks are merited and could help you perform better in the future.

Score 11–18 You can handle constructive criticism without feeling too stressed but are upset by unreasonable comments.

Score 8–10 Criticism pours off you like water from a duck's back. While this makes excessive stress less likely, it could also mean that you take insufficient notice of important criticism, and risk making similar mistakes in the future.

While you can't do much to change a critical boss or spouse, there is a great deal you can do to reduce the stress that unjustified and destructive criticism creates.

The first thing to decide is whether a critical comment has any merit. If it does, then be prepared to put aside hurt feelings and learn from what has happened. If undeserved, and intended only to wound, the critical comment is best ignored.

The problem is how to remain sufficiently objective, when stung by a criticism, to distinguish the helpful from the hurtful. Here's a technique which does just that.

The next time you feel stressed by criticism, whether at work or at home, jot down the remark on a piece of paper small enough to fit into the palm of your hand.

Now ask yourself five questions.

Does the critic deserve my respect? Your answer will depend on whether he or she is criticising from a background of superior knowledge, skill or experience. A professional motoring instructor who criticises your driving knows what he or she is talking about. But if somebody lacking such qualifications does the same then they probably do not.

Where no superior expertise exists, fold your little finger down over the paper. Now ask:

Is their criticism reasonable? Was it expressed in a way designed to point out and improve your performance, or was it merely an excuse to launch a personal attack? Was it stated calmly and coherently, or blurted out in a rage which took the remarks to extremes?

If you fairly regard the criticism as unreasonable, fold the next finger down over the paper. Now ask:

Is the criticism realistic? After a traffic accident made him late for work, Peter's boss angrily criticised him for unpunctuality. 'He refused to even hear my explanation,' Peter recalls. 'It was most unfair, since my time-keeping is usually very good.'

Any time you are blamed for something beyond your control, regard the criticism as unrealistic and fold down your middle finger. Now ask:

Is the criticism relevant? Critical comments intended to hurt or humiliate are rarely relevant. The critic launches an attack that has nothing to do with the issue in hand. After she had incorrectly collated an important report, Mary's manager launched a furious assault on her physical appearance, claiming that she took insufficient care over her grooming. Clearly this attack was designed to make her feel bad, rather than point out and correct her professional error.

If you can honestly say that a criticism is irrelevant, fold down your index finger. Finally ask yourself:

Is the criticism rational? Is it a fair and objective appraisal of *all* the relevant information? Irrational criticism is often motivated by envy, jealousy or ignorance. Such comments usually say more about the critic's problems than about your own alleged failings.

If judged irrational, fold your thumb over the paper, crumple it up, toss it away, and forget the criticism. The comments are clearly not worth further time or effort.

Destroying a criticism in this way helps banish painful emotions. Imagine your stress being discarded into the dustbin with the ball of crumpled paper.

But suppose not all the fingers can be folded down, because you have to agree that your critic's views should be respected, or that the remarks were reasonable, realistic, relevant and rational? The mere fact of reaching

74

such a conclusion makes the criticism helpful and constructive.

Reflect on how you might do or say things differently to avoid such criticism in the future. At the same time reduce your stress by taking the following steps.

1. Accentuate the positive

When reflecting on the criticism use the PIN approach. This stands for Positive/Interesting/Negative.

Start by considering all the *positive* features of the criticism. Next think about anything *interesting* that was said, whether or not positive. Only then should you dwell on the *negative* aspects of the situation. And even here you must review the event in a constructive manner.

Avoid falling into the trap of claiming, 'Yes, but I've always done it this way!' Even when such objections are valid, raising them in your defence inhibits further consideration of whether you could learn from a negative comment.

Change 'Yes, but . . .' to 'Yes, and . . .' Say to yourself: 'Yes, and I could change this . . .'

Even the most unwelcome and hurtful criticism may contain at least one positive feature. By finding and focusing on it, you achieve two important stress-control benefits. First, you make it more likely that something good can come out of an apparent setback; second, you make it more probable that the other person will be more receptive to your ideas, rather than becoming anxious and defensive.

2. Evaluate the criticism objectively

Once all the positive aspects have been considered, seek out any 'Red Buttons' triggered by the comments.

As I mentioned in Chapter 10, we all have Red Buttons: remarks, accusations, charges which have the power to trigger an emotional reaction out of all proportion to the actual criticism. Once a Red Button has been punched, it can arouse such powerful feelings – of anger, panic, outrage, guilt, jealousy, despair, envy, and so on – that we are no longer capable of thinking straight or forming rational judgements.

Never respond to a criticism in such a disturbed emotional condition, but postpone further internal consideration until you have calmed down.

3. See it as a criticism of the performance, not the performer

Even when we know a criticism is justified, it can cause such distress that we defend ourselves by switching off mentally, avoiding the issue or refusing to acknowledge that the comment was justified. By doing so, we fail to learn the lessons necessary for avoiding similar mistakes in the future.

If you feel stressed and angry, calm down physically using one of the relaxation or breath-control techniques described in later chapters. Then, when you feel calmer, take another minute to reflect on the criticism. This time, however, view it as a comment on what was done, rather than taking it personally.

If your critic was angry or upset, consider which of his or her Red Buttons you might have pressed to provoke this powerful reaction.

Such insights can help you to avoid a similar situation in future. They might also give you a winning edge in subsequent negotiations, since your critic has betrayed a potentially vulnerable spot in his or her make-up.

18

Coping With the Stress of Worry

Even people who appear confident and relaxed can suffer high levels of worry-related stress. Such worries may circle endlessly around your head or pop suddenly into your mind – often during the early hours – making you depressed and fearful. There are two main types of worry:

Acute worries These come unbidden to mind, perhaps as a result of something you've seen or heard that triggers a chain of negative associations, initially below the level of consciousness.

By the time you become aware of acute worries, the stress can be so overwhelming that it leads to what has been termed 'awfulising': making a major problem out of a minor difficulty by carrying the worry to absurd extremes.

Chronic worries These are never far from your thoughts, no matter how busy and distracted you keep yourself. They cast a pall of gloom over everything you do, however enjoyable those activities used to be.

When severe, they result in a condition known as *anhedonia*, an inability to find pleasure in anything. Anhedonia is a common symptom in depression.

When Worry Strikes

You are most vulnerable to both chronic and acute worrying in the hours before dawn. Napoleon once remarked he had 'yet to meet an officer with three o'clock in the morning courage'.

The cause is biological rather than psychological. Around this period of the day, physical resistance is at its ebb. Temperature and blood-glucose levels are low, the metabolism sluggish. Dangerously ill patients are more likely to die at this time than at any other.

Not surprisingly, your bodily state exerts a considerable influence over your mood. Worries about health, money, career or relationships chase uselessly around your head, driving sleep ever farther away.

Worry Solves Nothing

Most sensible people recognise that worrying is completely unproductive. Now a study at Columbia University has provided scientific evidence to support that common-sense belief. It showed that:

> Forty per cent of what we worry about never happens
>
> Thirty per cent of the problems are over and done with by the time we start to worry about them
>
> Twelve per cent of our worries are about non-existent health problems
>
> Ten per cent of worries are actually focused on the wrong things

Which leaves just eight per cent of worries worth bothering about!

No single approach to bringing worry stress under control is likely to work on its own. Experiment with the following, in conjunction with the rapid-relaxation, positive-mental-imagery and breathing techniques described later in this book. (See Guide to Techniques.)

What to do

This procedure is divided into seven practical steps. Use as many of them as are necessary to help you control worry stress.

Identify the eight per cent of reasonable worries by spending sixty seconds carrying out this Worry Test. Keep an eye on your watch and strictly ration yourself to fifteen seconds per answer.

Consider one particular worry and ask yourself:

1. How likely is it that this will happen? Rate this from 1 = Extremely improbable to 5 = Virtually certain.

2. How accurate is my information? Rate this from 1 = Highly dubious to 5 = Absolutely reliable.

3. Are there practical steps I might take to prevent it? Rate this from 1 = Many practical steps to 5 = No way of improving matters.

4. How serious are the likely consequences? Rate this from 1 = Not very serious to 5 = Catastrophic.

If your score was between 5 and 10, the worry is too trivial to waste further time on. A score above 16 suggests that the problem is so intractable, nothing you can do seems likely to improve matters, so you might as well stop worrying. If your score was between 11 and 15, worrying would seem justified, but only as a spur to action. Take practical steps to improve the situation by

> Finding out more about what is happening
> Developing a strategy for avoiding or lessening
> the consequences of what is happening

In addition, try one or more of these sixty-second stress-control techniques.

Step 1: Put your worries into perspective

When we are worried, things can quickly get out of perspective. A girl who had just finished her first year at university wrote the following letter to her father:

> Dear Dad,
> Just a line to let you know how I am getting along. Things are pretty good at the moment, and I am recovering well in hospital after my car

accident. It was foolish of me to drive when so drunk, I suppose.

I am afraid the police have decided to prosecute since I did so much damage to the Rolls-Royce which my car hit and wrote off. It was stupid of me to take my boyfriend's car without his permission and when uninsured.

The doctor says my broken left leg will mend fine, and the really good news is that my unborn child was unharmed. I had meant to tell you before about being pregnant. I am sure you will like my boyfriend and I hope you can meet him in about six months' time when he is released. We met at the drug rehabilitation clinic where they have, more or less, cured my heroin addiction. Although it now looks as if I have become an alcoholic.

Your loving daughter
Julie

PS None of the above is true. But I have just failed my first-year exams and hope this puts things into perspective!

Try using the same tactic yourself to deal with everyday worries!

Step 2: Deliberately exaggerate your worries

In some situations, taking a worry to absurd lengths actually makes it easier to deal with. This approach is not appropriate for all types of worry, especially those concerned with health. But with other worries, exaggerating the consequences to a ridiculous extent reduces their threat.

You may protest that this is already happening, as you imagine yourself getting into worse and worse trouble. But the essential difference is that the *absurd* image you conjure up must have little or no connection with reality.

For example, delayed by traffic on your way to meet an important but quick-tempered client, you start worrying about his angry reaction if you arrive late. Instead of fretting and becoming stressed, try taking the situation to extremes.

Not by picturing the client lodging a complaint with your boss, a black mark appearing on your file, your career being in jeopardy, with redundancy, disgrace and bankruptcy staring you in the face. Although fairly absurd, such imagery is too close to a possible reality to take the sting from the worry.

The image you should develop focuses on wildly absurd consequences. You might imagine your client so furious over your being ten minutes late that he attacks you with a huge axe the moment you enter his office. Continue to fantasise by picturing him chopping through furnishings as you dodge his blows. Picture your client growing horns, foaming at the mouth, his eyes bulging from their sockets in his demonic rage. Imagine his secretary pulling a lever to open a trapdoor which drops you into a pit full of alligators as she cries, 'So perish all who arrive late for a meeting!'

The more vivid and ridiculous you make this exaggeration, the greater its power to reduce stress by making your worries seem more silly than threatening.

Step 3: Create a mental barrier to worry

Whenever a worry comes into your mind, immediately think, 'Yellow unicorns,' picturing these mythical beasts as vividly as possible.

Since you can hold only one thought in conscious awareness at a time, focusing your mind on a totally different topic – and one that is most unlikely to arouse any worrying associations – creates a barrier to further worrying.

Having momentarily stopped the worry in its tracks, switch your attention to some task that is enjoyable and requires concentration. If this is impossible, start thinking about a pleasurable activity planned for later that day.

Step 4: Delay worrying for as long as possible

When the worry involves something which will happen at some time in the future, use 'Just-in-Time Worrying'. Tell yourself, 'I am right to be concerned. But since nothing bad is going to happen until tomorrow morning, that's when I'll start worrying.'

Step 5: Identify irrational thinking behind the worry

Some of our most stressful worries are caused by irrational ideas. Here are a dozen of the most potent. Although widely believed, each idea is false:

> I must be approved of and loved by everybody I know: family, friends and even casual acquaintances
>
> I must be unfailingly competent and perfect in all I do
>
> It is terrible if things, people or events are not as I wish them to be
>
> I must have somebody or something stronger than myself to rely on
>
> I am helpless and cannot control what I experience or feel
>
> Lasting relationships depend on my being unselfish
>
> People will reject me unless I continually please them
>
> If people disapprove of me, it means I must be wrong or bad
>
> Being alone is the worst thing that can happen. My happiness depends on others
>
> There is perfect love and a perfect relationship somewhere to be found
>
> My value as a person depends on how much I achieve
>
> The answer to all my problems is out there somewhere

If any of these ideas are causing you worry, try and

accept that they are totally untrue. See them for what they are, falsehoods often perpetuated by spouses, parents, teachers, preachers, even therapists, to gain power over you. Dismiss them, and the worries they generate, from your mind.

Step 6: Prevent early-morning worrying

Whenever possible, exercise before going to bed. People who work with their brains all day may feel intellectually exhausted without being physically tired. A brisk walk, jog, swim or aerobic session during the evening helps ensure a full night's rest.

Avoid drinking coffee or smoking before bed, since these arouse the nervous system and impair your ability to experience deep sleep. While an alcoholic nightcap helps some people sleep, avoid too much strong drink because it interferes with natural sleep patterns. Keep your bedroom cool and well ventilated, your bed snug and warm. Drink a glass of warm milk before bed. Milk contains the amino-acid L-Tryptophan, which stimulates the production of *serotonin*, a brain chemical involved in producing sleep.

If, after fifteen minutes of trying, you cannot fall asleep, get up and write notes about any worrying thought circulating in your brain. Now go back to bed. If you are still awake and worrying after another fifteen minutes, repeat the exercise. Continue until you fall asleep again within fifteen minutes of getting into bed. It is important to get up to write down your thoughts, so as to break the subconscious association between lying in bed and worrying. Writing worries down, a process known as 'Externalising', makes them easier to view in an objective light. Apply the Worry Test described above to see how valid they are.

Recall a time in the past when you felt extremely sleepy but had to fight off rest because of external demands, perhaps while driving a long distance or listening to a dull speech. Concentrate on this image and you will start to feel drowsy. Now tell yourself something like: 'Never mind about arriving at my destination on time. I must stop and take a nap,' or 'I don't care if the speaker does see me, I'm going to snooze.' After a few moments you will drift off to sleep.

If you still wake early and start worrying, tell yourself that this has little bearing on reality and is due to low blood-glucose levels. Reassure yourself that things will seem far less daunting when daylight comes. Focus your mind on any pleasurable activities scheduled for later in the day.

Step 7: Send your worries up in smoke

To avoid bringing work worries home, send them up in smoke, either literally or symbolically. If possible, write your main worries on a scrap of paper, then burn it. Tell yourself that, now that those worries have been reduced to ashes, they need concern you no longer. If such worries are unrealistic, their cremation can be regarded as the end of them. If not, wait until tomorrow before resurrecting them.

Where you can't physically burn your worries, imagine setting them alight and watching them disappear from sight, at least until the following day.

19

Controlling Your Stress by Controlling Your Breath

One of the first things that happens when we become stressed is that our rate and type of breathing changes. It may even cease momentarily.

If you held your breath when clenching your fist in the test at the start of this book, your response to any sudden stress is likely to be a held breath.

Your breathing may increase, from a normal rate of between twelve and sixteen breaths per minute. It may also become shallower, so that only the upper portions of your lungs are used. Rapid, shallow breathing is called *hyperventilation* and always occurs during panic attacks.

Whenever your breathing is inhibited and inefficient, stress will quickly rise above your PPSL. Full, efficient breathing, in contrast, ensures that your whole being – emotionally, physically and intellectually – is enhanced.

That is why we describe somebody filled with creative life energy as being 'inspired' or having an 'inspiration'.

How Breath Change Affects Your Body

The range of distressing effects caused by changes in breathing is seldom fully appreciated.

It includes: racing heart, chest pains, dizziness and faintness (especially in young people), anxiety, panicky feelings, an inability to concentrate, diminished intellectual and physical performance, disturbed sleep, nightmares, increased 'emotional' sweating beneath the arms and on the palms, sensations of unreality, disturbed vision, even hallucinations.

In people who are vulnerable to hyperventilation, it is frequently possible to provoke a panic attack merely by asking them to breathe rapidly and shallowly for a couple of minutes.

The Medical Consequences of Hyperventilation

All these damaging effects are due to faulty breathing creating an imbalance in the ratio of carbon dioxide to oxygen in our blood.

As is well known, we draw oxygen from the air when inhaling, and expel carbon dioxide, the waste product of metabolism, with each exhaled breath. These gases travel around the body in our bloodstream in a very tightly controlled balance.

By reducing levels of carbon dioxide in the arterial blood, hyperventilation creates a condition known as *hypocarbia*, in which the small carbon dioxide molecules are able to pass in and out of nerve cells (neurones) even faster than water. Even slight hypocarbia causes an immediate migration of carbon dioxide from the neurones. This triggers an increase in nerve-cell activity and electrical discharge in the associated nerves. At the same time, veins constrict, reducing oxygen supply to the brain and creating sensations of dizziness, faintness and unreality. One widely used first-aid treatment for panic is to breathe into and out of a paper bag. By rebreathing the carbon dioxide-rich exhaled air, the balance is restored and panic abates.

Stress-related hyperventilation triggers a vicious cycle in which rapid breathing produces distressing physical symptoms, and the anxiety these arouse causes a further increase in stress.

Holding your breath in response to stress leads to a rapid build-up of carbon dioxide, with equally distressing mental and physical consequences.

But these are not the only stress problems associated

with shallow breathing. Attached to your ribcage is the diaphragm, a domed sheet of muscle which acts as a flexible wall dividing the abdominal and chest cavities. Your diaphragm plays an important role in digestion and circulation, by preventing stomach acid flowing back into the oesophagus, and aiding the heart in pumping blood up from the legs, abdomen and pelvis.

When the diaphragm flattens and contracts during deep breathing, abdominal pressure increases. Together with the abdominal muscles, this creates an inflatable 'jacket' which helps support the lower back. A well-functioning diaphragm is able to make a significant contribution to your health, enabling you to combat stress more effectively. An inefficient diaphragm depletes your SRC reserves by undermining your physical well-being.

How do You Breathe?

Carry out this sixty-second examination the next time you are stripped to the waist.

Looking into a mirror, study your chest carefully while continuing to breathe normally. Notice which parts of your chest rise and fall with each complete breath.

Now place your hands on your breastbone, one above the other.

Inhale slowly and deeply.

Exhale.

What type of movement did you see and feel?

Did your upper or your lower hand rise farthest?

Keeping one hand on your breastbone, place the other against your back, reaching as far down between your shoulderblades as possible.

Inhale and exhale slowly and deeply once again.

Did you see and feel more movement in the upper or the lower portion of your chest?

Finally, place a hand low down on either side of your chest.

Inhale deeply as before.

Exhale.

Where is movement most noticeable this time: in the upper part of your chest, revealing shallow breathing, or down towards your abdomen, indicating deep breathing?

The distances may amount to only a few inches; but physiologically and psychologically, this makes a very great deal of difference.

Deep and Shallow Breathing

We can breathe in one of two main ways.

The first is by raising the chest wall using the intercostal muscles between each rib.

The second method is to flatten and contract our diaphragm, while moving the upper ribs and breastbone forward and upward to increase chest capacity.

In each case, a partial vacuum is created in the chest cavity, which draws air into the lungs.

If your ribcage moved mainly outward and upward, your breathing is costal.

If most of the work was done by your diaphragm and muscles forming the abdominal wall, your breathing is deep and efficient.

The Penalties of Shallow Breathing

Except when exercising vigorously, costal breathing is inefficient because most of the air reaches only the middle areas of your lungs, rather than the lower portions, which are richest in oxygen-absorbing blood vessels. Because of this, your body must work harder to achieve the required level of gas exchange. Since your oxygen requirement depends on how hard your muscles are working, costal breathing requires a greater number of breaths per minute than deep abdominal breathing. This faster, shallower breathing increases the risk of hyperventilation during stressful encounters.

To make matters worse, costal breathing is part of a primitive survival mechanism which evolved tens of

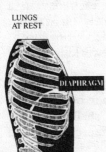
LUNGS
AT REST

Note position
of the diaphragm

DEEP
BREATH

The ribcage expands and the
diaphragm lowers, which can
more than double the volume
of air in the lungs

EXHALING TO
THE MAXIMUM

The ribcage is forced
down, the diaphragm
rises

**Efficient, abdominal breathing uses the diaphragm
to draw air into and expel air out of your lungs**

thousands of years ago, when all the dangers our an-
cestors faced were physical and the only options were to
fight or flee. This subconscious association means that
when you breathe using your ribcage only to draw air
into the lungs, physical tension rises sharply.

Deep or diaphragmatic breathing, by contrast, infuses
your blood with additional oxygen and stimulates your
body to release mood-boosting endorphins.

Because expansion and ventilation occur in the lower
parts of the lung, which are richest in blood vessels, we
can slow down our breathing and still achieve optimum
exchange of gases. Since we breathe like this when calm
and composed, breathing deeply reduces tension, aids
relaxation and creates a greater sense of control.

Check Your Breathing Regularly

Monitor your breathing several times each day in a variety of situations, such as immediately on waking, after commuting through congested traffic, during lunch, prior to a challenging meeting and while working at your desk.

This regular checking will help you to become aware of the way different situations affect your breathing. If you find you are constantly taking shallow, costal breaths, get into the habit of breathing more slowly and deeply.

In Chapter 24 I will be describing practical exercises for using abdominal breathing in a variety of stressful situations.

20

Massage Away Physical Stress

With your eyes closed and arms outstretched, try touching your two index fingers together.

Most people are able to do this without difficulty because sensors within each muscle provide the brain with information about its position in space and how much strain it is under. A muscle under needless tension is sending constant stress messages to the brain.

When muscles contract, their blood vessels are constricted and blood-flow decreases. This leads to a build-up of such waste products as carbon dioxide and lactic acid, while limiting the muscle's supply of oxygen. The result is yet more stress and increasing bodily distress.

Posture, Pain and Muscle Stress

Faulty posture, caused by sitting hunched over a desk or computer terminal for lengthy periods, results in muscle-cramping and fatigue. This situation will be aggravated if your diet is low in calcium.

Unfortunately, tension messages from affected muscles are often ignored until the discomfort becomes so great that it forces us to take notice of what is happening. By this time the pain and distress can be considerable, causing a corresponding increase in mental stress.

Muscle spasm

The most painful, and obvious, sign of muscles under excessive stress is a spasm. This happens when a group of muscle fibres contracts suddenly. Unless treated, the spasm produces knots of hard, tangled lumps known as *trigger points*, which limit movement and can be extremely tender to the touch. Having occurred once, spasms are more likely to happen again, leading to chronic discomfort.

Treating muscle spasm For a muscle spasm, cold is far more comforting than heat, so use an ice-pack made by wrapping cubes or crushed ice in a towel (to protect the skin from frostbite). Cold numbs your nerves, reducing the pain signals which are causing blood vessels to contract. These vessels can then dilate, increasing blood-flow to the affected muscles. Cold also diminishes the build-up of fluid in the muscle, another source of pain.

Keep the pack on for twenty minutes, then off for twenty minutes, alternating over a period of hours. After forty-eight hours, change the cold compress for a warm one.

You may also benefit from massaging the painful area for five to ten minutes. I shall explain how to do this later in the chapter.

Analysing Your Muscle Awareness

The following exercises will help you get back in touch with your body so that stress signals can be detected far earlier and prompt remedial action taken. Remember that the faster you move to reduce stress, the easier and quicker it is to treat.

The results of these exercises will also help you to identify the best techniques for treating bodily stress.

You will need a pillow and a quiet place where you can lie, full-length, on the floor. Loosen tight clothing and remove your shoes before starting.

Every exercise you can perform without discomfort or undue effort scores 0. If an exercise cannot be done at all, score 10 points. Between these extremes, award yourself points according to how easy or hard you find each exercise.

A Word of Caution

If you have high blood-pressure, recently underwent surgery or have any other reason to doubt the wisdom of carrying out these exercises, seek advice from your doctor before doing the tests.

Checking Your Neck and Shoulder Muscles

Exercise 1
Turn your head first to the left and then to the right, moving as far as possible in each direction without causing yourself any discomfort. Notice whether you find it more difficult to turn your head in one direction than the other.

Exercise 2
Bend your head forward and rotate it in a complete circle, first clockwise then anticlockwise. To stretch these muscles fully, try to bring your head as close to your chest and shoulders as possible while rotating.

Exercise 3
Standing upright, reach behind your shoulder with one hand and up your back with the other so that your fingers can touch. If this proves too difficult use a mirror to see how far apart your fingertips are.
If you scored 4 or more on any of these three exercises, refer to Techniques Eight, Thirty-Nine and Forty.

Checking Your Back Muscles

Exercise 4
Lie face-down with a pillow under your stomach and your hands by your sides. Now try and lift your upper

back and shoulders, without pushing up with your arms, keeping the lower part of your body flat on the floor.

This time there is no score if you are able to keep yourself raised for ten seconds. Award 5 points if you are only able to hold the position for five seconds, and 10 points for anything less.

Exercise 5

Remove the pillow and place your hands, palm-upwards, beneath your thighs. Keeping your legs straight, raise them as high as possible and time how long you are able to hold them in that position without any effort or pain. Score in the same way as for your upper back.

If you scored 4 or more on either of these exercises, refer to Techniques Seventeen and Twenty-Four.

Checking Your Stomach Muscles

Exercise 6

Lie down on your back and place your hands behind your head. Bend your legs, keeping your feet flat on the ground. Now, without moving your legs, try and touch your elbows to your knees. Do not attempt to hold this position but immediately return to the lying position.

Score on how easily and comfortably you were able to carry out this exercise. If you could touch your knees without any effort there is no score. If you were unable to do so, or felt very uncomfortable when attempting the action, score 10 points.

If you scored 4 or more on this exercise, refer to Technique Sixteen.

Checking Your Wrist Muscles

Exercise 7

Stretch out each hand in turn and rotate your wrists, first clockwise then anticlockwise. Score as above, depending on the ease and comfort with which this exercise was performed. If you had no difficulty in rotating either hand there is no score. If one or both felt stiff, or the action caused discomfort, then score up to 10.

If you scored 4 or more on this exercise, refer to Technique Forty-One.

Checking Your Leg Muscles

Exercise 8
While standing, place your feet 12 ins apart and attempt to touch your palms – not just the tips of your fingers – to the floor between them.

Score as previously, according to the ease and comfort with which this exercise was carried out. If you were able to swing down easily and without discomfort there is no score. If you were unable to touch the floor at all, even with your fingers, then score 10 points.

Exercise 9
Stand on tiptoe, lifting yourself up on to the balls of your feet, then walk around the room, keeping your legs straight. Try to do this for thirty seconds. If you achieved it without effort there is no score. Give yourself 5 points if you experienced slight discomfort after fifteen seconds, 10 points if you were unable to continue with the action for a full thirty seconds.

If you scored 4 or more on either of these exercises, refer to Technique Nine.

Checking Your Ankle Muscles

Exercise 10
Stand upright and place your right hand on a chair or table for balance. Now lift your left leg as high as possible while rising on to the ball of your right foot. Hold this position for a slow count to three then lower your left leg and place your right foot flat on the floor.

Now raise your left leg once more, but this time out to one side of your body. As you do so raise yourself on to the ball of the right foot. Hold this position for a count to three as before.

Finally, raise your left leg out behind you while rising on to the ball of your right foot for the same count to three.

Repeat all three of these exercises, this time raising your right leg while rising on to the ball of your left foot.

The scoring system is, as in all the other exercises, no points if the exercise is easy and comfortable to perform, up to 10 points should it prove impossible.

If you scored 4 or more on this exercise, refer to Techniques Forty-Four to Forty-Six.

The higher your score on any of these exercises, the more important it is to work on those stressed muscles following the techniques suggested.

Massaging Away Muscle Stress

Massage is one of the most powerful antidotes to physical distress and tension that exist. The first thing a hurt child does is seek comfort by gently rubbing the afflicted area. When applied correctly, massage does far more than relieve pain. Your hands have the power to reduce bodily stress and to promote mental and physical well-being.

A full body massage from a qualified practitioner will take between thirty and sixty minutes. If you can do so, make this a regular part of your stress-control programme.

It is possible, however, to produce beneficial results in as little as sixty seconds, provided tension is dealt with promptly.

Every so often, check the different muscle groups for

unnecessary stress. Use a trigger, such as the phone ringing, finishing a piece of work or being stopped at a red light when driving, to remind you. Spend a few moments focusing on each part of your body in turn, moving from the feet and ankles, up the leg to your lower back, shoulders, neck, jaw, forehead, arms, wrists and fingers. If you notice any tension, massage the affected muscles using the techniques described in Chapters 23 and 31. Although it is best to massage your skin directly, good results can still be achieved through light clothing.

At the end of each day, spend slightly longer massaging away any remaining tensions. The best time is while having a bath or before going to sleep.

Types of Massage

You will be using three different types of massage:

Effleurage is a French word meaning 'skimming-over'. This involves a stroking motion which is firmer on the *upward* stroke (in the direction of the heart) than on the return. Effleurage can be performed with both hands simultaneously or with one hand after the other.

Petrissage, another French word, means 'kneading', and describes a movement performed by pressing the muscles firmly against the underlying bones using the palm of your hand. This can be done by one hand, using a continuous motion, or by alternating hands.

Deep-friction massage is carried out making small, circular movements using one or more fingers pressed firmly against the muscles, so that the skin moves with the hand. The skin should move with your fingers rather than have them slide across the surface.

Preparing for Your Massage

When massaging away stress at home, apply some lubricating oils first. I will describe the most effective types to use for various forms of stress in the next chapter.

Preparing your hands Before starting your massage, always warm your hands by rubbing them together briskly, then shaking them as if drying off water. Oriental specialists claim this 'charges' the hands with healing power, the left hand (ying) being negative and the right (yang) positive.

Where there is time, enhance your massage with the following warm-up exercise:

Lie on your back and stretch your arms over your head. Take a deep breath and, while exhaling, stretch out your arms and legs. Inhale and relax. Repeat twice. If space permits, roll on to your right side, arms and legs stretched out in front of you. Lifting your left arm, circle slowly to the right side, allowing your left leg to follow the movement around. Continue so that the gentle momentum rolls you on to your other side, bringing your right arm over to the new starting position. Repeat two or three times.

A Word of Caution

Massage is normally a safe and extremely beneficial method for reducing excessive stress; but there are a number of points to bear in mind.

Any persistent pain is a warning that something is not quite right with your body and should be taken seriously. Always consult your doctor about any chronic pain or one that is causing you concern.

Seek medical guidance about self-massage if you are recovering from a serious illness, following surgery, or while you are running a temperature.

If you are pregnant, avoid massaging your stomach, although other parts of the body are safe. This restriction also applies if you have had abdominal surgery.

When in doubt, always seek the advice of your doctor.

21

Scents Which Banish Stress

Aromatherapy is based on the principle that scent can both heal the physical body and promote emotional well-being. Although known to the Egyptians more than four thousand years ago and widely used by eastern physicians, aromatherapy has only recently become accepted in the west.

This therapeutic art involves aromatic extracts from wild or cultivated plants gathered at full maturity. Some of these essences are inhaled, whilst others are used directly on the skin. A few drops sprinkled into your bathwater will envelop you with soothing, stress-reducing fragrances.

Scents also act as powerful memory triggers. For many people a whiff of sea or country air will evoke a whole host of happy, relaxing memories.

Try sniffing a pleasant fragrance, such as almond, while recalling some happy memory. Smelling the same scent the next time you feel stressed or miserable will bring this memory vividly to mind, so raising your spirits.

Preparing Essential Oils

For massage, use a dilution of three drops of essential oil to two teaspoonfuls of carrier oil. If you want to make up a three-ounce bottle, use thirty drops of your chosen essential oil(s).

The carrier oil serves as a vehicle for the blend of essences so that they can be applied to the skin. Avocado or wheatgerm oils provide a skin-nourishing carrier. Because these are rather heavy on their own, you may want to mix in a lighter oil, such as almond, olive, soya or sunflower-seed.

Almost all vegetable and essential oils become rancid when they oxidise, producing an unpleasant odour in vegetable oils and a loss of freshness in the essential oils. As this process cannot be reversed, be sure to keep your oils in dark, air-tight bottles, preferably well filled. A few drops of wheatgerm oil, which is rich in vitamin E and acts as a natural antioxidant, can also be added. Sandalwood oil is the best fixative, although you can also use cedarwood. Fixatives make the scent last longer so that the oil does not lose too much fragrance as it evaporates.

A good blend for stress is: one drop basil, two drops geranium, two drops lavender.

When blending, fill your bottle with the carrier oil or oils, and then add the essences by drops. Cap the bottle and shake it gently.

For inhalations, add eight to twelve drops to a bowl of hot water. For a facial steamer, add four to six drops to the hot water. For relaxing bathing, add between three and five drops of essential oil to your bathwater.

A Word of Caution

Essential oils should be used with discretion, since they have a powerful effect. With the exception of lavender, no essential oil should be applied directly to the skin.

Essential Oils for Controlling Stress

There are a great many different essential oils, and it's worthwhile experimenting to find those most personally beneficial in controlling stress. Here are eight which I have found most helpful:

Bergamot This oil comes from the rind of a fruit, resembling a pear-shaped orange, which grows in Italy.

Named after the city of Bergamo in Lombardy, it is used to scent Earl Grey tea. Stimulating, uplifting, antiseptic and antidepressant, it is excellent for treating general anxiety. Do not apply to the skin before going out into sunshine or exposing yourself to a sun lamp.

Camomile Gentle, relaxing and soothing, this is one of the oldest known medicinal herbs. With an apple-like fragrance, it was called *kamai melon* ('ground apple') by the Greeks. The type commonly used in camomile tea is known as German camomile.

Clary sage Warm and euphoric, this oil induces a sense of well-being. The plant resembles common sage, but its blue flowers are smaller. The name 'clary' is derived from the Latin *sclarea*, meaning clear. A native of Syria, France, Italy and Switzerland, this plant was used in ancient times. A clear oil, with a sweet, slightly nutty aroma, clary sage blends well with lavender, juniper and sandalwood. Clary sage is an excellent general tonic and pick-me-up. In fact, a few drops in your bath can lead to a mild form of intoxication. It is also excellent for lifting depression.

Lavender A relaxing anti-bacterial oil, it takes its name from the Latin *lavare*, 'to wash'. Lavender was a favourite bath perfume among Romans. Although grown in all European countries, its main commercial producer is France. It is good for reducing panic and calming frayed nerves. Its antiseptic properties also make it invaluable for treating many skin problems, including insect bites and stings, acne, boils, eczema and dermatitis. Lavender oil can be used to treat – but *not* prevent – sunburn. For muscle aches and pains, apply it in a concentration of two to four drops per three ounces of carrier oil. A lavender-scented bath last thing at night will help ensure restful sleep.

Melissa This lemon-scented herb is found in Europe, Middle Asia and North America. Its leaves are small and serrated, the flowers white or yellow. The name comes from the Greek for 'bee', an insect that is especially attracted to the plant. The eighteenth-century herbalist

Joseph Miller wrote: 'It is good for all disorders of the head and nerves, cheers the heart, and cure the palpitation thereof, prevents fainting and melancholy'. Like many essential oils, melissa has a joyful effect on the spirit.

Neroli An oil extracted from the blossoms of the bitter orange (*Citrus aurantium*). The name probably comes from the sixteenth-century Princess Anne-Marie of Nerola, who first used it to perfume her gloves and bathwater. Its most common use is in eau de Cologne, where it blends with lavender, lemon, bergamot and rosemary to form the classic toilet water. Neroli is one of the most effective sedative/antidepressant oils, and may be used for insomnia, anxiety and depression.

Peppermint Soothing, stimulating and refreshing, peppermint was very popular among the Greeks, who used it to flavour wines and sauces, as well as in medicines. While North America produces more peppermint oil than any other country, that cultivated in Italy, Japan and Great Britain is generally considered of superior quality. Recent research has shown peppermint to be an excellent stimulant. One sniff is often all it takes to feel mentally and physically aroused. So powerful is the effect that some Japanese companies now introduce occasional puffs of peppermint into the air-conditioning to keep employees alert.

Ylang-ylang This sensual, soothing, euphoric oil comes from the yellow flowers of a tree which grows sixty feet high and is cultivated in Java, Sumatra and Madagascar. The name 'ylang-ylang' means 'flower of flowers', and it has an exotic, very sweet scent reminiscent of jasmine and almond. Ylang-ylang lowers blood-pressure, slows a rapidly beating heart (*tachycardia*) and is excellent for combating anger and tension. However, the oil should not be used undiluted, since it may then lead to headache and nausea.

These eight are, of course, only a tiny portion of the vast number of essential oils available for aromatherapy which have a wide range of health-promoting properties.

22

Beating Start-the-Day Stress

Your day can be stressful before you even get out of bed. One reason is that we often move directly from deep sleep to full wakefulness, leaping up as the alarm sounds or racing to make up for lost time after lying in for longer than was sensible. This creates an unnecessary level of arousal, needlessly using up your reserves of Stress Resistance Currency. By starting the day in a more relaxed state, you will find it far easier to remain at your Peak Performance Stress Level when facing the challenges ahead.

The following techniques will help you start off at that level: relaxed yet energetic.

Technique One: For a Stress-Free Start to Your Day

Before getting out of bed, prepare your system for the transition from sleep to action by gently stretching your muscles.

Stretch the muscles of your right foot, by flexing the toes towards the shinbone as you inhale slowly and deeply. Hold that breath for a moment then, while exhaling, curl your toes.

Do this action three times.

Now repeat the exercise with your left foot.

Finally, lengthen your body in a long, languid movement like a big cat stirring lazily from sleep.

Push downwards with each foot in turn to stretch your leg muscles.

Stretch your arms one after the other above your head while exhaling.

Slowly get out of bed and stand upright with both feet on the floor and your weight evenly balanced.

Take two deep breaths.

Curl your toes inward while inhaling and flex them while exhaling.

Repeat this action three times.

You are now ready to start the day.

Try and carry the sensation of relaxed alertness which this exercise has produced by moving slowly but purposefully through your daily routine.

Technique Two: For Giving You Greater Energy

As well as boosting your energy levels at the start of a new day, this technique can be used whenever you start to feel:

> Mentally and physically exhausted
> Lacking in energy
> Unable to concentrate

You may find this technique easier to perform if you close your eyes. If the outside air is fresh and clean, position yourself close to an open window.

Plant each foot firmly on the floor, at a comfortable distance apart, so that your weight is evenly distributed.

Inhale deeply while slowly raising your arms in front of you and over your head, and stretch your palms towards the ceiling.

As you breathe in, picture the air as white light, which flows through your entire body, starting at the top of your skull and cascading downwards to exit through your feet. If you notice any areas of special tension, try and imagine this purifying light being directed to those muscles and dissolving away the stress.

As you exhale, rock gently from side to side, by shifting your weight between your right and left foot, while slowly lowering your arms.

Repeat this action three times.

Try to carry these feelings of relaxed alertness into your everyday activities. Use this technique any time during the day when you start to feel your energy levels under attack from stress.

Technique Three: Use Clary Sage to Stimulate Mind and Body

Add extra zest to your system by adding a couple of drops of clary sage essential oil to warm – not hot – water and inhaling deeply while gently splashing the water on to your face.

Technique Four: Take Ginseng to Increase Resistance to Stress

Research suggests that ginseng, an ancient Chinese and Korean tonic, can enhance our ability to resist stress while increasing alertness and generally improving performance. Ginseng is readily available at all well-stocked health-food shops and most large pharmacies.

Technique Five: Use Music to Manage Your Moods

Listening to the daily litany of disaster and death which comprises the morning news can prove an extremely stressful way to start your day. Unless it is part of your job, there is no reason – other than habit – to tune in to misery the moment you wake.

It is far more sensible to lift your spirits by playing a favourite piece of music. The ability of music to create a mood is well known to everybody from generals – who use martial tunes to stir troops to battle – to lovers, who choose romantic rhythms when making love.

Start your day by listening to music that makes you feel lively, optimistic and joyful.

Unexpected changes in tempo make the heart beat faster, whilst melodic changes create a pleasurable shiver down the spine. Many find, for example, that Bruckner's *Ave Maria* sends a tingle down the spine, while Prokofiev's *Fifth Symphony* causes their heart to race.

If you feel increasing tension in your solar plexus or neck, the music is arousing. Brisk-tempo, arousing music helps prepare you for a challenging day ahead.

If your breathing becomes slower and deeper while listening, then the music is relaxing you. So if you are tense and need to unwind, select music that creates feelings of relaxation.

Flute, harp, piano and string ensemble pieces are generally more soothing than vocal ones. The ideal tempo for relaxation is slightly slower than your normal, resting heart-rate. Choose sonatas and symphonies played *adagio* (slow tempo) or *andante* (moderately slow). They will reduce your blood-pressure and slow your heart by encouraging it to beat in time with the music.

Suitable classic pieces include: Bach's *Brandenburg Concerto No. 4*, second movement; Bach's *Orchestral Suite No. 2* (Saraband); 'Venus' from Holst's *Planets*; Ravel's *Mother Goose Suite*, first movement.

For many people, the most soothing sounds are recordings of nature: gently flowing streams, birdsong, a breeze rustling leaves, waves lapping gently on the shore and whale songs all inspire tranquillity and a sense of being one with nature.

This combination of exercises, aromatherapy, ginseng and mood music will help you start your day with ample reserves of Stress Resistance Currency.

Continue managing stress in this practical way as you travel in to work, or during your working day, using the techniques described in the next chapter.

Combating Travel Stress

The daily commute in to work, usually on congested roads or crowded public transport, is highly stressful for the majority of people. Reserves of Stress Resistance Currency are squandered before you even start to confront the major stressors of the day.

Fortunately there are some one-minute stress-management techniques to ease the mental and physical effects of all types of travelling. Some can be used while still in your car or on the bus; others must await your arrival.

Travelling, by car, plane, train or bus, often involves sitting for long periods without adequate support for your neck. As a result, tension quickly develops in the muscles of the neck and shoulders, leading to stiffness, headaches and increased bodily stress.

Because your neck is the body's point of balance, train yourself to become conscious of its position at all times and always to hold your head and neck as upright as possible. Inflatable neck-rests, which are easy to carry around, offer useful additional support.

Technique Six: For Reducing Your Stress While Travelling

Inhale deeply while gently raising your shoulders in a shrug.

Hold the tension for a moment, then exhale, lowering your shoulders and allowing them to sag. As you breathe out, imagine the tension flowing out of your neck and shoulder muscles.

Repeat this action three times.

Now spread and stretch your fingers, breathing in deeply while doing so. Exhale and relax your fingers. Feel any stresses in your hands, wrists and forearms flowing from your body.

Repeat this action three times.

Make fists, inhaling as you tighten the muscles of both hands simultaneously. Hold this tension for a moment and then release, exhaling while doing so. As before, imagine stress in the hands, wrists and forearms flowing away from the muscles with your exhaled breath. Allow your hands to rest loosely in your lap.

Repeat this action three times.

Stretch your neck first by turning your head gently from side to side and then by nodding. Do all this slowly, allowing time for the muscles to stretch at the furthest limit of each movement. When exercising your neck, always make sure your movements are smooth and gentle. Avoid any abrupt motion which might cause strain.

Carry out these exercises at regular intervals when travelling. They can be done easily if you are a car passenger. When driving you will, obviously, have to stop the car. By preventing these muscles from getting over-stressed in the first place, you will help conserve your SRC.

Whether or not you feel able to carry out this and other techniques described below while travelling on public transport depends on how embarrassed you feel by the presence of fellow-passengers. I have no problems about this when flying or on a train. On most occasions my actions provoke neither interest nor comment. The few times people have asked what I am doing, I explain how beneficial these actions are in controlling stress. Nearly always, the response is an interest in being taught the technique!

Technique Seven: For Improving Your Alertness When Travelling

This exercise increases alertness by enhancing the flow of blood to your brain. As well as helping you remain vigilant while travelling, the technique can improve your powers of concentration during any type of intellectually demanding work.

Combined with Technique Two, it can bring your mind into a high state of alertness, making it an ideal preparation for a difficult negotiation or any form of mental challenge.

Resting your left elbow in your right hand, pull it gently towards your right side, keeping your head steady and looking straight ahead. Inhale deeply while performing this action.

Hold the tension for a moment, then release the arm, allow it to rest lightly in your lap. Exhale, and feel the tension flowing away from your left arm and shoulder.

Repeat the action with your right elbow.

Place both palms on your chest, with elbows pointing out to the sides.

Circle your elbows three times clockwise and then three times anticlockwise.

Finally, roll your head, gently and smoothly, first clockwise then anticlockwise. While doing this, try to relax your neck to such an extent that your head feels like it could almost fall off.

Technique Eight: For Reducing Stress in Your Shoulders and Neck

Let your head fall forward.

Place the fingertips of both hands at the point where your neck and upper back meet, to locate the protruding bone. This is your seventh cervical vertebra, the focus for a complex network of nerves in your back, head and neck.

Using the middle and index fingers of one hand to

apply moderate pressure, circle this bone twenty times. Use the effleurage massage technique described in Chapter 20. Make sure your flesh moves beneath your fingertips, rather than allowing the fingers to slide across your skin.

Next, locate two slight depressions at the very base of your skull. The main tendons controlling your head movements can be felt next to the depression. This area is especially vulnerable to stress and should be soothed using deep-friction massage.

Perform this massage by starting at the seventh vertebra and working slowly upwards along the tendons.

Technique Nine: For Reducing Stress in Your Legs

The muscles in your legs assist in returning blood from your feet to your heart by squeezing and compressing the blood vessels.

This 'muscle pump' is essential to maintaining healthy circulation and ensuring an uninterrupted flow of oxygen-rich blood to the brain. Guardsmen who must stand at attention for long periods sometimes faint because the muscle pumps are no longer able to aid blood-flow. The faint is a natural protective response, which restores cerebral blood-flow. Sitting in an aircraft or car seat for lengthy periods can also reduce the efficiency of these muscle pumps, making you feel increasingly sluggish and uncomfortable.

The following technique is excellent for destressing these vital muscles on arrival at your destination.

Stand upright. Bend your left knee and extend your right leg behind you. Your arms should remain relaxed at your sides.

Raising and lowering your right heel, make a series of small, bouncing movements. After ten bounces change and extend your left leg.

Now sit in a chair, stretch out your right leg and point your toe, then rotate your ankle for ten seconds.

Do this six times, three each way, then repeat using your left leg.

In addition, you may find the following techniques helpful if severely stressed by your journey.

Holding on to a chair with your left hand, stand with your feet turned out sufficiently to provide good balance.

Swing your right leg to the right, keeping it slightly bent. Your supporting leg should be straight.

Without pausing swing your right leg back in front of your body, with a fluid movement, brushing the ground lightly with your foot while doing so. When touching the ground, your foot should be slightly turned out.

Swing your leg back to the right again, once more brushing your foot against the ground.

Do this ten times then repeat with your left leg.

Technique Ten: For Reducing Your Over-all Stress

This is an excellent way of reducing muscle stress throughout your entire body, after travelling in fairly cramped conditions by car or plane.

You will also find it helpful when obliged to remain sitting or standing for lengthy periods.

This technique can only be done somewhere quiet and private where it is possible to sit or lie down and stretch your arms and legs to their full extent. Use it after arriving home, or at your hotel, but never within two hours of eating a large meal, since by diverting blood from your digestive system it can cause indigestion.

After loosening tight clothing, sit or lie down comfortably.

As you stretch out in the chair, on a couch or bed, or even on a well-carpeted floor, imagine all the stress in your muscles flowing out of the body.

Breathe in while stretching and out again as you release the tension.

Inhale, slowly and deeply, through your nostrils. *Never* hold your breath while stretching. Ideally this technique should be performed with eyes closed so as to help you concentrate on the way your muscles are responding.

Stretch fully and freely, extending your arms above your head with your feet pointing forward.

Hold this tension for five seconds and then release.

Repeat this exercise three times.

Technique Eleven: Aromatherapy For Stress Reduction When Travelling

Apply a few drops of bergamot, melissa or peppermint essential oils to your handkerchief and inhale whenever you start feeling stressed. They will clear your head and help you feel more relaxed.

24

Combating Hassle Stress

Major stress difficulties are often an accumulation of the multitude of trivial irritations, frustrations, disappointments, setbacks and aggravations that make up the everyday hassles of life.

Although individually their drain on your reserves of Stress Resistance Currency may be slight, when present in sufficient numbers and over a long enough period they can result in the psychological bankruptcy of Burn-Out Stress Syndrome.

In this chapter, I describe techniques for use whenever you feel that life's hassles are threatening to push you over your Peak Performance Stress Level.

Technique Twelve: For Combating Your Day-to-Day Stress

When you are learning this technique the sessions will take longer than one minute to complete. Once mastered, it can produce beneficial reductions in mental and physical stress in as little as sixty seconds. You can also use it for longer periods to produce an even deeper state of relaxation.

The technique involves deliberately tensing and then relaxing all your major muscles. During training you do this by working on various muscle groups in turn, following the method described below. Then, when used to combat daily stress, *all* your muscles are tensed and relaxed simultaneously.

While using this technique it is important to avoid

any pause between an inhaled and an exhaled breath. Breathe continuously and evenly, drawing the air deep into your lungs. Each time you exhale repeat the word 'Calm' silently to yourself. Imagine all your stress flowing out with the expelled air.

When practising, sit or lie in a quiet room where you are not going to be disturbed. Remove your shoes and loosen any tight clothing. You may find it easier to concentrate if you close your eyes and/or play soothing music.

The first step is to remember how to tense each of your major muscles. This is made easier by remembering the phrase '*A* *s*oothing *f*eeling, *m*y *b*ody *h*as *p*eace.' The first letter of each word represents a group of muscles.

A is for arms, wrists and hands
Tense the muscles in your forearms by extending your hands at the wrists. Bend them back, and feel tightness building in your forearm.

Hold this tension for a slow count to five.

Allow your hands to flop right out.

Feel all the tension flowing away from them.

Notice the difference between tension and relaxation in these muscles.

Keep your breathing slow and regular. Remember not to pause between inhaling and exhaling. Repeat the word 'Calm' silently to yourself as you breathe out.

Next tense the muscles in your biceps by attempting to touch the *back* of your wrists to your shoulders.

Hold for a slow count to five before allowing your arms to drop limply into your lap, if seated, or to rest loosely at your sides if lying down.

Notice the difference between tension and relaxation in your biceps.

Tense your triceps by stretching your arms out as straight as possible.

Hold for a slow count to five.

Let your arms flop down by your sides.

Notice the difference between tension and relaxation in your arms, hands and wrists.

Spend a few moments focusing all your attention on these muscles, while continuing to breathe slowly and smoothly. Repeat the word 'Calm' on each exhaled breath as you feel your arms becoming heavier and warmer.

S is for shoulders and neck

You tense these muscles by shrugging your shoulders as hard as you can.

At the same time press your head back firmly against the chair or bed.

Hold this tension for a slow count to five.

Let your shoulders drop and go limp, your head resting back against the support.

Your breathing must remain steady and smooth.

Notice the difference between tension and relaxation in your shoulders and neck. Feel these muscles becoming warmer, heavier and more and more relaxed.

F is for face

Our facial muscles are often under considerable needless tension as we struggle to conceal emotions from others. It is important to work on these muscles carefully and thoroughly.

Start by tensing the muscles in your forehead.

You do this by frowning hard and screwing up your eyes.

Hold this tension for a slow count to five.

Now relax. Smooth out your brow. Let your eyelids rest lightly together.

Breathe slowly and deeply, remembering to repeat the word 'Calm' silently on each exhaled breath.

Notice the difference between tension and relaxation in your forehead.

M is for mouth and throat

Still working with your face muscles, press the tip of your tongue firmly against the roof of your mouth. While doing so clench your jaws tightly.

As before, hold this tension for a slow count to five.

Relax. Let your tongue rest loosely in your mouth. Your lower jaw should hang loosely, with your teeth slightly parted.

Spend a few moments focusing on your throat and jaw, noticing the difference between tension and relaxation in these muscles.

B is for body, chest and abdomen

The muscles of your chest and abdominal wall can be tensed and relaxed simultaneously.

Do this by taking and holding a deep breath – the only time during this exercise that you should stop breathing. At the same time pull in your stomach, flattening muscles as though anticipating a blow.

Feel the tension building up in your chest and abdomen.

Hold for a slow count to five.

Expel the air from your lungs in a loud gasp. At the same time let your abdomen go limp and flop right out.

Return to smooth, continuous breathing, repeating the word 'Calm' each time you exhale.

H is for hips, thighs and calves

The final group of muscles is those in the legs.

To tense these, stretch your legs, point your toes and squeeze your buttocks tightly.

Hold this tension for a slow count to five.

Relax completely.

Continue to focus on your breathing and notice the difference between tension and relaxation throughout your body. Notice that, as your relaxation deepens, your body becomes warmer and warmer, heavier and heavier.

Enjoy the pleasant sensation created by destressing all

the major muscle groups. You should feel very deeply relaxed, calm and at peace with yourself.

This exercise requires around five minutes to perform, and you should try to lie still for a further five to ten minutes afterwards.

The final part of your training consists of simultaneously tensing as many of the major muscle groups as possible.

While seated, clench your fists, trying to touch the back of your hands to your shoulders while shrugging hard. At the same time frown, screw up your eyes, press the tip of your tongue to the roof of your mouth, clench your jaws, take and hold a deep breath, flatten your stomach, stretch and point your legs, while squeezing your buttocks tightly.

Hold all this tension for a slow count to five.

Now let go. Flop right out.

Smooth your brow; let your mouth hang loose; arms and legs go limp like a rag doll. Imagine you are a puppet whose strings have all been cut.

Check that your breathing is slow, deep and regular. As you breathe out, feel any remaining stress flowing from your whole body.

The final P in your memory phrase stands for

Picturing

Having relaxed your body, you must calm your mind by conjuring some tranquil scene.

You might imagine yourself lying on a sun-warmed tropical beach or in a lush meadow beside a gently flowing stream. At first this image is likely to be vague and easily disrupted by intrusive thoughts. With practice, however, most people achieve a vivid and enduring image.

If worrying ideas come to mind while you are picturing your relaxing scene (this is very likely during early training sessions), imagine writing those thoughts with a stick on the wet sand at the edge of the tide. Now watch as the ocean laps in and obliterates your problem. As the last trace is washed away, you will experience relief from the worry. Alternatively, imagine the distressing thought written on a sheet of paper, caught on the breeze and blown higher and higher until it finally vanishes out to sea or over the hills.

If you have worries that you have difficulty talking over with friends or family, picture a small, friendly creature emerging from the nearby greenery and approaching you timidly. Imagine yourself befriending this animal, which can understand everything you say to it. Confiding all your fears and doubts to this creature while you are mentally and physically relaxed helps make them seem less daunting and puts difficulties into a clearer perspective. Although this may sound odd, many find the image helpful and comforting.

I term these *sensualisations*, rather than 'visualisations', since it is important, when creating your personal paradise, to involve as many of your five senses as possible.

If you are lying on a beach, *hear* the sound of waves gently uncurling on the sands, *smell* the fragrance of wild flowers, *feel* the warmth of the sun on your body, *taste* the salt on the sea breeze, *see* the palm trees overhead.

Do not worry if, at first, it proves tricky to hold a vivid mental picture for more than a few seconds. This is normal. Your ability will rapidly improve with practice. You may also find it difficult to use all five senses. Some aspects of the scene, such as sights and sounds, will prove easier than others to imagine. Once again, this develops in time.

When you feel confident with this technique use it several times a day to banish the stress created by everyday hassles.

Go somewhere quiet and private and sit or lie down as comfortably as possible.

Relax quickly by tensing *all* the muscle groups as described above. Hold for a slow count to five. Relax. This takes ten to fifteen seconds. Spend your remaining time creating a tranquil scene to calm the mind.

To monitor your success, take your pulse before and

after using the technique. With practice you should experience a drop of around ten heartbeats per minute.

You can use the technique before and/or after some stressful encounter, or as a means of destressing yourself two or three times a day.

If you have to return to a mentally and/or physically demanding activity you'll need to wake yourself up again at the end of the session. Here's what you should do:

Close your eyes and clench your fists tightly.

Briskly bend your elbows and stick your arms out, either in front of you or to the sides.

Inhale deeply.

Open your eyes and exhale.

It is very important to keep your eyes closed right up to the moment you breathe out.

Now go about your daily routine, in a calm and relaxed manner.

Technique Thirteen: Warming Away Your Stress

There are many stressful situations in which it is impossible to use the relaxation techniques I've described. When waiting to speak before an audience, or during an interview, for example, there is no way you could start tensing and relaxing your muscles.

Under these circumstances, this technique comes to the rescue. It is a means of relaxing deeply and rapidly which is completely unobtrusive. You could carry it out entirely surrounded by people without anybody being aware of what was happening.

When we are stressed, blood is diverted away from the small vessels directly beneath the skin and sent deeper into the muscles in preparation for vigorous action. This is why people often go pale with shock.

By consciously reversing this natural process, you can lower arousal and reduce stress. You can do this by learning how to make one hand warmer than the other. There is nothing mystical or even especially difficult about such a feat, although it does take practice.

What happens is that, as you become more relaxed, blood is automatically transferred from the muscles to the blood vessels directly beneath the skin. This blood is closer to your body's core temperature of 37° than the skin, which becomes warmer as a result.

If you want to monitor your progress while training, use a small alcohol thermometer to record temperature changes. Alternatively, use one of the new liquid-crystal thermometers, which change colour to indicate changes in temperature. Biodots and stress cards, sold by many chemists, work on the same principle. These are less helpful, since they may not be sufficiently sensitive to measure small changes of temperature.

With only a little practice you should find it possible to raise the temperature of one hand by two or three degrees through an effort of will. The amount of hand-warming possible depends on your initial skin temperature. A chilly hand will obviously warm more than one already close to your core body temperature.

There are three ways to warm your hand and I suggest you practise each of them to discover which works best for you.

Stare at your dominant hand (your right if you are right-handed), and imagine it becoming warmer and warmer. Just by concentrating on the idea of heat flowing into your fingers and palm, you may achieve a significant rise in temperature.

Imagine holding your dominant hand before an open fire. Feel the heat from these flames warming your skin and raising your temperature.

Place the palm of your dominant hand close to but not touching your cheek. Your cheek naturally radiates a good deal of heat. Feel this gently warming your hand.

Keep breathing slowly and deeply while carrying out your chosen technique. Allow the feeling of warmth from your palm to spread down the arm and through your whole body, until you feel deeply relaxed.

Hand-warming is a skill that takes regular practice

to master. But once perfected you will have added an important weapon to your stress-fighting armoury.

Technique Fourteen: Breathing Away Your Stress

Deep, rhythmical breathing reduces stress as effectively as rapid, uneven breaths increase mental and physical arousal.

To achieve stress-free breathing, your weight should be distributed evenly through your spine and legs while you are standing; through the spine and pelvis if you are sitting. Disturbing this balance creates a barrier to efficient breathing.

If you are in the habit of leaning on the wheel of your car when driving, or across your desk while you are working, most of your weight will be taken by your elbows and shoulders. This makes them tense and unnecessarily involved in the breathing process. A hunched posture also pushes your digestive organs upward, limiting the movement of your diaphragm and lower ribs.

Once poor posture has become a habit, breathing efficiency is significantly reduced and your capacity for resisting stress is impaired.

Use some kind of external event as a reminder to check your posture and breathing several times an hour. This might be answering the telephone, finishing a task or fetching a coffee. Focus attention on the way you are sitting or standing and, if necessary, alter your posture so that your weight is distributed more evenly.

Sit upright.

Close your eyes.

Place one hand on your chest and the other on your abdomen. Breathe smoothly, slowly and deeply through your nose.

Pull in your abdomen as you exhale, if necessary using your hand to push down your stomach.

As you inhale, become aware of the muscles forming your abdominal wall pushing outward.

Continue for thirty seconds.

After checking your posture again, resume the task at hand.

In just half a minute your reserves of Stress Resistance Currency will have increased significantly.

Practise for a few minutes each day until this becomes your normal pattern of breathing, whether you are sitting, standing or lying down.

Technique Fifteen: For Reducing Emotional Stress

Arguments, unforeseen bad news, unexpected setbacks and aggressive encounters can produce acute stress. This sudden surge in arousal has to be dealt with promptly to prevent it undermining your confidence and performance. This technique allows you to do just that.

Find somewhere quiet and private.

Loosen your tie and open the top buttons of your shirt or blouse.

Sit or lie back. Use Technique Twelve first to reduce physical stress.

If possible use a massage oil containing either lavender or neroli essential oils. Half a teaspoonful is usually sufficient to cover your face and neck, although you may require more if your skin is especially absorbent (which becomes more likely if you work in air-conditioned offices or have just taken a hot bath). While this oil is beneficial, it is not essential to the technique.

Using both hands, fingertips closed and touching, start under your chin.

Apply firm, gentle strokes, moving out towards your ears. Your wrists should remain supple and your hands pliable. Using only the fingertips, gently massage your cheekbones, travelling up each side of your nose to your forehead.

Massage your eyebrows then circle your eyes, moving up your nose and across your forehead as far as the hairline.

Repeat this soothing action from the bridge of your nose to your forehead several times.

Stroke down your nose, chin and throat in one continuous line.

Complete the massage by gently stroking your face and neck.

Now return to your work feeling calm, relaxed and free from stress.

Technique Sixteen: For Combating Stress in Your Lower Back

After a stressful day, you often find your lower back knotted with pain despite the fact that those muscles were not directly implicated in your daily hassles. By strengthening the muscles of your abdominal wall you will provide additional support for your lower back as well as greater protection for your digestive tract, liver and kidneys.

The following technique not only reduces stress but improves your digestion.

Place your hands on your hips, with fingers touching the groove which runs either side of the spine.

Apply deep-friction massage along the groove.

Raise your hands half an inch up the body and repeat.

Continue as far up your back as is comfortable.

Apply a kneading movement to the flesh around the small of your back, as if gently but firmly kneading dough.

Technique Seventeen: For Combating Stress in Your Stomach

The first warning that you are becoming adversely stressed is frequently a disagreeable sensation in the pit of your stomach, due to the release of adrenaline. This can cause a rapid spiral of increasing stress, which adversely affects your whole body.

Lie on your back with your knees bent, bringing the heels as close as possible to your buttocks.

Placing your hands behind your head, raise yourself slowly as far as you can.

Doing this only once is commendable if you have allowed the stomach muscles to weaken. If you are able to do so, repeat up to six times for even greater benefit.

Breathe in as you sit up and exhale as you relax down again.

Do not worry if you are unable to complete this technique on the first few tries. Persevere and it will become manageable.

25

Controlling Concentration Stress

Working for long periods on intellectually demanding tasks can be far more stressful than you realise. We may become so deeply absorbed in the complexities of some task that signals warning of rising stress are ignored until it is almost too late. By this time stress has risen above your PPSL, adversely affecting efficiency.

Use these techniques to combat excessive stress whenever you are faced by:

> Tasks requiring lengthy periods of intense
>   concentration
> Intellectually demanding problems and decisions
> The need to remember facts and figures against
>   a deadline

Technique Eighteen: For Increasing Your Mental Energy

The inside of your nose is lined with spongy tissue which constantly distends and constricts. As the tissue expands in one nostril it contracts in the other. As a result, you will always find it easier to breathe through one nostril than the other. Prove this for yourself by closing each nostril in turn with your finger. Because this pattern alternates every ninety-five to 120 minutes, if you perform the same test in a couple of hours' time the chances are that the situation will have reversed.

Studies suggest that when the air is flowing freely through our right nostril we feel more active, assertive and alert. When air-flow is easiest through our left nostril we feel intuitive and more inwardly directed.

The right–left nostril differences are also reflected in the way our body works. Research indicates that a right-nostril air-flow stimulates internal processes such as digestion.

These changes are thought to be linked to differences in the way the left and right hemispheres of the brain function. As is well known, in the majority of right-handed people the left side of the brain is specialised for speech, hearing, logical analysis and objective reasoning. The right hemisphere, by contrast, is more concerned with fantasy, intuition, dreaming and non-logical reasoning.

This technique uses alternate nostril breathing to help balance the right and left hemispheres of the brain, so enhancing intellectual performance.

Sit comfortably with your head and neck fairly straight.

Breathe slowly and gently, drawing the air deep into your lungs.

Press your right thumb gently against your right nostril and breathe out slowly through the left nostril. At the end of that exhalation, and without any pause, breathe in again.

When your lungs are filled, lift your thumb to open the right nostril, this time closing your left nostril using the middle finger.

Slowly exhale, then breathe in again through your left nostril.

Repeat the procedure until you have completed nine breaths through each nostril.

Technique Nineteen: For Reducing Mental Stress

With both hands, gently stroke your scalp from hair-line to back using straight and circular movements alternately.

Spreading your fingers across the scalp, apply sufficient pressure to move the skin slightly across the skull beneath, as if shampooing your hair.

Apply fingertip massage to centre line of your scalp, using small, circular movements.

Place three fingers of each hand on either side of your neck and stroke from the spine outwards, using firm pressure. Start the movement immediately beneath your skull and continue moving downwards, until the whole neck has been massaged.

Repeat all these actions three times, making certain to keep your movements gentle and rhythmic.

Technique Twenty: For Soothing Stressed Eyes

This technique can be used to reduce stress after

      Prolonged work at a computer terminal
      Reading or preparing lengthy reports
      Lengthy periods of study
      Working under bright, artificial light
      Fine work that puts a strain on the eyes

Place your index fingers either side of your nose, directly below the inner ends of each eyebrow.

Apply a firm pressure for ten seconds.

Using a circular movement, massage very gently around the eyes using your fingertips.

Repeat three times.

Using your thumbs, apply a gentle pressure to the inner portion of the eyebrow arch, moving outwards from the bridge of your nose.

Place your hands on your brow with the fingertips just touching. Now, using a series of gentle, circular movements, massage your whole face, starting at the temples and slowly moving your fingertips first across the temple and then down and around your cheekbones until they reach your nose. Repeat the action three times.

Complete this massage by rubbing your hands briskly

together then placing them over your eyes and forehead. Feel the warmth from your hands flowing into your eyes and face, easing away any remaining stress.

Technique Twenty-One: For Combating Concentration Stress

After warming your hands by rubbing them together, place them both over your face, palms covering the eyes and fingers crossing on the forehead. Avoid pressing against the eyeballs. Relax, shut your eyes, and feel your eyeballs sinking ever more deeply into their sockets.

After a few seconds, stroke your fingertips outwards from the centre of your forehead.

Repeat three times.

Place the first two fingers of each hand on your temples and rub gently, using circular movements. After a few moments, move your fingers a little way up or down the temple and repeat this movement.

Technique Twenty-Two: Using Peppermint to Increase Alertness

Peppermint oil has been shown to combat fatigue and improve alertness. Place a few drops of the essential oil on your handkerchief or use a special dispenser, sold under the brand name Kiminto, which can be found in most chemist's.

Alternatively, place a few drops of peppermint oil in warm (not hot) water and splash over your face.

At the end of a long period of intensive brainwork, put a couple of drops into warm bathwater and inhale the refreshing fumes while relaxing.

Use Chinese or Japanese oil if possible, as this is far richer in menthol, the active ingredient, than the American oil.

26

Dealing With Posture Stress

A great deal of avoidable stress arises from poor posture.

Think of your body as a complicated machine, moved by rods (bones) and springs (muscles and tendons). Because of the way it has been designed, this machine is only able to operate without stress – efficiently – over a limited range of movements. Outside this range it still functions, after a fashion, but every action becomes less efficient and creates higher levels of stress.

When walking, for example, most people lift their knees too high, pulling, rather than pushing, themselves along. This movement increases stress by inhibiting the body's natural forward motion.

The secret of stress-saving posture is to move from the middle of your body, or solar plexus.

Your solar plexus is located about halfway along an imaginary line passing directly beneath the centre of your chestbone (the sternum) and your spine. On a fairly slender person this is approximately four inches inside the body. The solar plexus, a massive communications centre, is surrounded by many vital structures, including your major blood vessel, the aorta.

Nerves radiate from here to arteries, veins, muscles, joints, heart, lungs, stomach and bowels. In this way the solar plexus acts as a sort of telephone exchange, receiving and sending messages between your tissues, your organs and your brain. As every boxer knows, the solar plexus is such an important centre of nervous control that a punch here causes loss of consciousness.

As a command post for the autonomic nervous system

your solar plexus helps regulate stress via the fight-or-flight mechanism. In this way it exerts either a positive or negative influence on every part of your body, including your brain.

When moving without undue stress, bodily tension is focused on the abdomen, your body's natural centre of gravity and the stable pivot around which other parts move. Professional dancers learn how to move from their 'centre' in such a way that the rest of their body remains relaxed and fluid. They achieve this by means of an upright, yet never ramrod, posture, and by maintaining good balance so that their weight is always evenly distributed. Keeping their shoulders relaxed and drawn back with their heads held up completes the centring. I shall describe how you can achieve the same balance in a moment.

Assessing Your Posture

The next time you go walking on a damp, sandy beach, take the opportunity to study your footprints.

If you can't wait until then, a messier alternative is to coat your feet with water-soluble paint and stand on a sheet of white paper.

Examine your footprints carefully.

Are they even, indicating balanced weight distribution, or do they roll to one side?

Do you favour one foot more than the other? Uneven distribution of weight can lead to aching legs and lower back, as other muscles strain to compensate for your poor balance.

Notice which foot is normally under the least pressure and make a deliberate effort to push it more firmly against the ground.

As a further check on your posture, stand with your back to a wall, feet hip-width apart and heels against the wall. Sway back against the wall.

Your shoulders and buttocks should make contact at the same moment.

When one shoulder or buttock makes contact with the wall first, your posture is twisted to that side.

If your shoulders touch first, your upper spine is unnaturally arched backwards, a condition known medically as *kyphosis*. If your buttocks make contact before your shoulders, the spine curves too far forward, *lordosis*. This is likely to cause low-back pain.

The hair on the back of your scalp should just brush against the wall. If the back of your head touches the wall, nod forward slightly.

Once you have achieved correct posture, move away from the wall and practise maintaining this relaxed stance while moving around by using the following technique.

Technique Twenty-Three: For Preventing Posture Stress

Stand upright and relaxed.

Tuck in your tail and lengthen your entire spine so that it is straight. This action will pull in your stomach.

Keep your buttocks taut and flatten your stomach by pulling in your abdominal muscles. This simple procedure alone will greatly reduce the risk of stressful lower-back pain.

Raise your ribcage by lengthening your waist, in the same way that you might extend an accordion. Let your shoulders drop down and keep them relaxed.

Imagine being a puppet with strings attached to each ear. These strings are drawn upward with even tension, raising your head so that your chin stays parallel with the ground.

Be careful not to tilt your head back; this leads to stiffness in the neck and shoulders.

Imagine a pivot running through your ears. Let your head fall forward on this pivot.

Now picture your head being gradually drawn upward

again. As you raise your head, simultaneously pull back your shoulders and straighten your spine.

Practise regularly, until this becomes your normal posture when standing and moving around.

Become aware, while practising, of unnecessary stress anywhere in your body. Although there will be increased tone in certain muscles, you should never feel uncomfortable or strained.

When walking around, keep your weight slightly forward and move with a flowing stride, swinging your legs from the hips. Imagine being pushed forward by a giant hand pressing gently but firmly on your behind.

Because a well-balanced posture reduces stress by preventing avoidable muscle strain, always 'ground' yourself after rising to make a speech in public. Spend a moment distributing your weight evenly, with your feet set a comfortable distance apart. Concentrate on making firm contact with the floor.

Technique Twenty-Four: For Banishing Stress When Sitting

Watch how people sit and you'll quickly realise that the vast majority adopt a needlessly stressful posture which, by straining muscles around the spine, leads to lower-back pain. The two most frequently observed faults are slouching, causing unnatural curvature of the spine; and leg-crossing, which twists the spine and impairs the circulation of the blood.

When sitting down always make sure your lower back is well supported, if necessary by placing a small cushion between your lower back and the chair.

Never sit in the same position for too long. Get up and move about several times each hour.

If you are typing, change your copy from one side of the machine to the other from time to time. Make certain that your desktop and other working surfaces are at the correct height, so that you are able to work without stooping forward.

While driving, sit near enough to the wheel so that your legs are not completely extended on the pedals. Once again, make certain your lower back is fully supported at all times.

At least once an hour, allow yourself a one-minute stress break.

For the first fifteen seconds, get back in touch with your body. Focus on each of your major muscle groups in turn: ankles, legs, lower back, shoulders, chest, neck, face, arms, wrists and hands. As soon as your attention is directed towards a particular muscle you will immediately know whether it is under excessive stress. When a problem is found, deliberately tense that muscle, using the technique described in Chapter 24.

Hold that tension for a slow count to five, then relax. Allow the muscle to flop right out and feel it becoming warmer and heavier.

Stretch deeply, raising your arms above your head. If possible carry out these actions standing by an open window or in fresh air.

Finish by shrugging hard three times to loosen any stress in the shoulders and neck.

Now you are ready to return to work with your reserves of SRC considerably increased.

Technique Twenty-Five: For Banishing Stress When Standing

If your legs are aching due to long periods of standing, for example at a workbench or behind a counter, here's an excellent way to free those muscles from unwanted stress.

Sit down and bend the right leg, leaving your foot flat on the ground.

Starting at your ankle, apply firm, deep strokes, moving your hands up towards your knee.

Rub firmly on any areas where tension is detected.

Grasping your Achilles tendon between your thumb

and fingers, massage by moving your fingers and thumb in opposite directions.

Now repeat the massage for your left leg.

By using these techniques regularly, you will prevent many of the aches and pains resulting from poor posture that can leave you so drained by the end of a working day.

27

Controlling Emotional Stress

In addition to the techniques for controlling emotional stress described below, keep in mind these general strategies.

Anticipate potentially stressful encounters and relax beforehand using one of the techniques described below

When faced with an emotionally fraught situation, speak calmly and stay as relaxed as possible. Others are more likely to mirror your response and calm down. By becoming anxious or angry you raise the emotional temperature, needlessly increasing the stress of that encounter. Do not allow other people to wind you up. Remember that, by doing so, they are actually robbing you of precious Stress Resistance Currency. Ask yourself whether you are really prepared to pay such a high price for losing your temper

If you feel upset, recall a recent occasion when something pleasurable happened, such as an unexpected compliment, a pay rise or the attainment of an important goal. This memory will lift your spirits and help banish the stress caused by disappointment, rejection, frustration or anger.

Make others feel important and they will go out of their way to help you

Technique Twenty-Six: For Controlling Emotional Stress 1

With practice, this technique can be carried out with equal ease standing, sitting or lying. At first, practise while lying down on a firm surface.

You may find this more comfortable if you place a small pillow under your neck. Stop immediately if you experience any discomfort.

Flop your shoulders like a puppet whose strings have been cut.

Smooth out your brow. Let your tongue rest loosely in your mouth, your teeth slightly apart.

Inhale. Flatten your diaphragm by pushing out with your lower ribs.

Imagine inflating a beach ball inside your abdomen, through a hole in your navel. Feel the ball growing larger and larger as air is sucked deep into your lungs.

To check that you are breathing correctly, place your hands, fingertips just touching, on your stomach. As your diaphragm flattens, your fingertips should be pulled apart.

Continue for one minute, keeping your breathing slow and deep.

An alternative is to lie face-down, legs comfortably apart, toes pointing outwards.

Fold your arms, resting your hands on your upper arms, and position them beneath your chest to prevent it touching the floor. In this posture you can only breathe using your diaphragm.

Inhale slowly through your nose by drawing down your diaphragm. If this action is carried out correctly you will feel your stomach pressing more firmly against the floor.

Now breathe out slowly and notice your stomach rising from the floor.

Continue to breathe in this way for sixty seconds.

Repeat several times a day, for a week or so, until you have got into the habit of breathing abdominally.

This will ensure that, even when stressed by an angry confrontation, your body and brain receive their full supple of oxygen-rich blood. Sustained deep breathing will also keep your anxiety levels low and easily managed.

Technique Twenty-Seven: For Controlling Emotional Stress 2

Emotions, especially those we have to bottle up, increase stress in several ways, the most important being by causing a change in the way we breathe.

Typically, the abdominal muscles become tense, pulling breastbone and ribcage downward. Now, whenever we take a breath, our shoulders and neck muscles have to work harder to overcome this force.

The result is fast, shallow breathing, with an increased risk of hyperventilation. Smokers are especially at risk, because they get into the habit of sucking air into their lungs using the muscles of the face, throat and upper limbs rather than the diaphragm.

This technique is especially helpful if you become highly stressed

> When swept by powerful emotions
> By having to bottle up painful feelings
> When obliged to deal with hostile or difficult
> people

Abdominal breathing should be mastered well in advance of any confrontation. This technique can also be used to reduce excessive stress immediately after any emotionally charged encounter.

When stressed, your stomach accumulates tension. Place your hand on a baby's stomach when he is crying and notice how fast he relaxes. Cats and dogs too become more relaxed when their stomachs are gently rubbed.

Lie down and slightly bend your legs.

Place your right hand on your stomach, just below the navel, and your left immediately above the navel.

Applying moderate pressure, circle your hands slowly and rhythmically clockwise, following the direction of digestion in the colon.

After fifteen seconds, cross your hands so that they make contact with opposite sides of the body.

Draw your hands firmly together, reducing the pressure gradually, so that when they meet in the middle the fingers are lightly stroking your skin. Repeat six times.

Now focus on your solar plexus.

Picture a shaft of golden sunlight flowing into this area and warming it pleasantly.

You are able to regulate this imaginary heat very precisely, to achieve the degree of warmth that feels most comfortable.

Do not become concerned if, at first, plexus-warming is hard to achieve. You may even find your midriff starting to feel slightly chilly. If this happens, or if you suffer some other mild discomfort, simply stop this part of the technique for the moment. Let a short time pass and try again. With practice you will find it far easier to direct stress-dissolving heat into the solar plexus.

Should this continue to cause you problems after three attempts, then set it aside – at least for the time being – in favour of one or both of the following two techniques.

Technique Twenty-Eight: For Controlling Emotional Stress 3

This is an ancient Chinese breathing technique called *Qigong* (pronounced 'chee-goong').

Stand upright, with your feet sufficiently far apart to ensure a good balance.

Keep looking straight ahead as you exhale.

Breathe in slowly while raising your arms above your head. Follow the stretch through, by rising on to tiptoe at the full extent of your reach. Feel the stretch going right down to your ankles.

Imagine a silver thread passing through your spine and lifting you still farther upwards.

Continue inhaling while stretching higher and higher.

At the peak of your lift, start to exhale slowly, allowing your arms to float gently down to your sides as you do so.

Push your palms down and flex your wrists at the end of your exhaled breath.

Repeat three times.

Technique Twenty-Nine: For Controlling Emotional Stress 4

As I explained earlier, many people get into the habit of holding their breath when they are suddenly stressed.

However unexpected the challenge, it is essential to continue breathing slowly and deeply in order to remain in control of the situation.

Sit or stand comfortably.

Inhale, counting slowly and silently up to six. Exhale, counting back from six to nought.

Be careful not to hold your breath between each inhalation and exhalation.

As you inhale, imagine crystal-clear fluid entering your body and helping to cleanse away all traces of stress.

As you exhale, imagine all the stress flowing out through your nostrils.

Repeat five times.

As you reach zero on your final exhalation, feel a sensation of calmness and control flood through your body. Carry this feeling of tranquillity into your next activity.

28

Controlling the Stress of Flying

These days more and more of us are having to make frequent, often lengthy, flights. Apart from any anxiety you may feel about flying – stress which is best controlled using rapid-relaxation and visualisation techniques – air travel is itself a stressful experience. You spend hours in a cramped position; breathing dry, stale, recirculated air; eating reheated meals; and, perhaps, drinking a large amount of alcohol; while crossing time zones disrupts your biorhythms.

In a study of eight hundred frequent travellers crossing multiple time zones, ninety-four per cent were found to have suffered jet lag; for almost half, the consequences proved severe. Ninety per cent reported feeling sleepy and fatigued on arrival, and remained so for several days. They felt wide awake at night but often dozed off during the day. Poor concentration affected seventy per cent, slowed reflexes sixty-five per cent; fifty per cent reported greater irritability; and forty-seven per cent complained of upset stomachs.

What Goes Wrong

One of the problems in flying is that cabin air is dehydrating and often of poor quality. And the longer your flight, the more the air deteriorates. The main loss is among negatively charged ions, resulting in an excess of positive ions. By stimulating your body's production of a hormone called *serotonin*, these electrically charged particles increase irritability, moodiness or lethargy.

The famous mistral, a cold, dry, wind found in southern France, contains a high proportion of positive ions and exerts a malevolent influence over all exposed to it. Negative ions, which are plentiful high in the mountains, among pine forests, at the ocean, near waterfalls and beside fast-flowing streams or rivers, produce a tremendous sense of energy and well-being.

Unfortunately, hotels, cinemas, offices, departure lounges or aircraft, which are enclosed, carpeted and air-conditioned, are naturally low in negative ions. The more people there are the scarcer these mood-enhancing ions become.

Oxygen is pumped through aircraft cabins from the front, which means flight-deck crew, first-class and business-class passengers enjoy the best atmosphere, whilst those seated towards the rear inhale staler air.

On business trips of more than two hours' duration, when your alertness on arrival could mean the difference between closing or losing a deal, it pays to travel business- or first-class. In addition to more room and better air, your ticket allows you to use less crowded lounges offering cleaner, fresher air and a more restful environment.

Unless you smoke, avoid the rearmost seats when flying tourist-class. Non-smokers should always travel as far away from the designated smoking zones as possible. Sitting just a few rows forward of smokers leads to your absorbing significant quantities of noxious fumes.

When travelling tourist-class, aim to spend a few minutes every hour as far forward in the aircraft as you can. In a jumbo jet use the toilets immediately aft of business or first class.

In a moment I shall be providing specific techniques for controlling the stress of flying, but first here is some general advice.

What You Can Do

In the air

Avoid alcohol and drink plenty of water. Those free glasses of champagne may seem tempting, but when flying on business they are best avoided.

For one thing alcohol of any type is a diuretic, which means you will want to pay more visits to the lavatory, with a consequent increase in the rate of dehydration. Remember that the dry air of cabins is already stressing your system enough, without adding to the difficulties by drinking alcohol. Fizzy drinks, whether champagne or Coke, are best avoided too. Because cabins are not pressurised to ground level – being in an aircraft is like being on top of a fairly high mountain in terms of air-pressure – gases expand. This means that any part of your anatomy that is able to swell – such as your guts and blood vessels – will do so. Drinking the carbon dioxide from carbonated drinks only makes matters worse.

For the same reason you should always loosen tight clothing. Where possible, it is far better to forget fashion and dress in the loosest-fitting clothes you can find. The less constricting they are the more comfortable you will feel on a long flight, and comfort should always be the flier's first priority.

One executive I know, who makes transatlantic crossings several times a month, wears a jogging suit on to the flight, taking her business clothes in a carry-on bag. Shortly before landing she changes in the lavatory in readiness for the first meeting.

Because your feet are going to swell, wear loose-fitting shoes or slippers. Most airlines provide these free of charge to first- and business-class passengers. But I prefer to bring along an old pair of carpet slippers. Not only do I know they will be comfortable, but their familiarity is somehow reassuring. They are a touch of home in an otherwise alien environment. If you don't fancy the idea of carting slippers in your briefcase, then an old pair of thick socks does just as well. These have the additional advantage of keeping your feet warm when sleeping through a night flight.

If you want to sleep, then avoid a high-protein meal and eat lots of carbohydrates instead. These stimulate the production of sleep-inducing chemicals in the brain. A meal of pasta, for example, provides energy for an hour or so then prepares your body for rest. For an evening meal choose the vegetarian menu or leave your meat.

If you want to stay awake, eat lots of protein: fish, meat, eggs, dairy products and beans, but avoid too much carbohydrate. By stimulating your adrenal glands, protein provides you with several hours of high energy.

After a night flight, request a high-protein breakfast from the cabin staff, or take along your own protein-rich snack of cheese, nuts, beans or chickpeas.

Tea and coffee contain substances called methylated xanithines, which help combat jet lag. This group of chemicals includes caffeine (found in tea, coffee, cola, chocolate), theobromine (found in coffee) and theophylline (found in tea).

For maximum benefit when flying across time zones, I advise you to drink no tea or coffee on the day before your flight. This will help clear your system. Drink two or three cups of tea and/or coffee on the morning of departure when flying west or in the evening before your flight if flying east.

Take regular exercise, to prevent your legs becoming cramped and to assist the work of the muscle pumps. Stand in the aisle and slowly raise and then lower yourself on your toes, ten, twenty or thirty times, changing your weight from one leg to the other.

On arrival

In a city, walk to the nearest park or green space. If it has a fountain or large area of open water, so much the better. In the countryside, climb a hill, or look for running water. By the ocean, stroll along the beach.

In your hotel room, open the windows whenever possible. If unable either to open a window or to leave your room take a warm – not hot – shower. Showers generate plenty of negative ions.

Many professional travellers now carry a portable ioniser to improve air quality in their hotel rooms. Smaller than a paperback book, these negative-ion generators can be used in almost any country provided you carry mains adaptors. Ionisers reduce physical stress caused by air-conditioning, prevent headaches, ensure a sound night's rest and boost energy levels.

The techniques described below will help to ensure that you arrive in the best mental and physical condition to conduct your business successfully.

Technique Thirty: For Increasing Alertness in the Air

This should be carried out once each hour on daylight flights. When flying at night, do it before going to sleep and immediately on waking.

If possible this exercise should be performed standing, to ensure your chest and abdominal muscles can expand freely.

Move as far forward in the aircraft as you are able.

Inhale deeply and smoothly through both nostrils. Feel the air being drawn deep into your lungs.

Hold that breath for a slow count to five.

Breathe out slowly. While doing so imagine the cramp and fatigue flowing from your muscles with the exhaled air.

Repeat five times.

On arrival at your destination carry out one or more of the following three techniques.

Technique Thirty-One: For Combating Stress After Flying 1

Standing a short distance away, place your outstretched right hand on a wall at shoulder height.

Stretch your right shoulder joint by turning your upper body slightly to the left. Inhale while holding the position.

Exhale and turn your body further away.

Repeat ten times.

Change sides and complete ten more inhalations and exhalations.

Technique Thirty-Two: For Combating Stress After Flying 2

Lie face-down and slide your elbows under your body, raising it slightly. Keep your hands in contact with the floor.

Your back, buttocks and legs should remain relaxed, as you rest your weight on your elbows.

Slowly and calmly, breathe in and out six times.

Technique Thirty-Three: For Combating Stress After Flying 3

Lie face-down with your arms at your sides.

As you start to breathe in, begin raising your arms towards the ceiling, keeping your elbows bent.

Provided you can do so without discomfort, bring your arms right over your head and back to the floor.

Time your movements so that they are completed at the same moment your inhalation ends.

Reverse the action, concentrating on achieving a slow, smooth, even exhalation as you lower your arms to your sides.

Try and make each exhalation longer and slower, while inhaling at whatever rate you find most comfortable.

Before long you will have trained your body routinely to breathe in this slow, stress-reducing manner in any situation.

29

Combating Stress Before it Arises

Preventing excessive stress from arising is more effective than coping with its effects.

Sometimes, of course, our stress levels rise so sharply that no preparation is possible. Frequently, however, we are able to predict which activities are likely to prove stressful and prepare for them in advance.

The approach described here is an elaboration of the sensualisation technique described in Chapter 24.

Sensualisations, so named because you should use as many of your senses as possible when creating them, allow you to destress situations before tackling them in real life, so making it easier to remain at your PPSL throughout the event.

To understand the power of sensualisation, try the following experiment.

Imagine holding a ripe lemon in your hand. Feel the texture of the fruit beneath your fingers. Hold it close to your nose and smell the sharp scent.

Now see yourself using a sharp knife to cut a thick wedge. Watch the stainless steel blade of the knife slice into the bright yellow fruit.

Imagine the sound as it cuts into the fruit.

Feel the lemon's resistance to the blade.

Observe a fine spray of juice spurting from the blade as the cut is made. Watch juice running down the knife and on to your fingers.

Picture putting that slice to your lips.

Run your tongue along the peel. Taste the juice on

your lips. Put the lemon into your mouth and suck on it.

As the tart taste of juice reaches your tongue, feel your cheeks curl and your lips pucker.

If that image was sufficiently vivid, your mouth will now be filled with saliva.

Merely imagining yourself cutting and sucking that lemon, you triggered a powerful bodily reaction.

This is not the only physical reaction that mental imagery can produce. Research carried out during the 1930s by Dr Edmund Jacobson demonstrated that if you merely imagine lifting a heavy weight with your right hand, the muscles in your right arm will show increased activity.

You'll find it easier to develop a sensualisation if your mind is quiet, your body relaxed and your eyes closed. This reduces the risk of interference from unwanted thoughts.

Before any sensualising activity set yourself goals that are both specific and realistic.

If, for example, you wanted to sensualise a potentially stressful confrontation with your boss, it would not be enough to set as your goal 'being more assertive'.

Translate that general aim into specific actions and results. How, exactly, do you want to behave? What kinds of things do you want to say and do? What would constitute realistic outcomes of such a meeting? Less work, promotion, a pay rise?

Setting yourself clear goals is important when using sensualisations, since they provide a means by which to measure your achievements.

Technique Thirty-Four: Controlling Stress Using Sensualisations

Sit or lie down comfortably and loosen any tight clothing.

Take a deep breath, hold it for a few seconds, then let it go.

148

Take another, hold it again. This time release the air with a 'Haaaaaaaaaaa' sound.

Focus on your breathing. As you inhale, say to yourself, 'I am,' and as you exhale say, 'relaxed.'

As you say 'relaxed', sink more deeply into the chair, rug or bed. Allow each and every part of your body to be drawn farther down . . . down . . . down into the support.

Feel your mind slowing.

As you inhale, imagine breathing in a warming glow of relaxation. Each time you exhale, picture all your tensions, fatigue and frustrations being expelled from your body.

Continue doing this for a few seconds.

Imagine a well, filled with crystal-clear water, extending from the top of your skull to the base of your spine. Picture a gold coin dropped into this well.

As you exhale, see the coin drifting slowly through the liquid and reaching the bottom of the well at the very moment you have completed that exhalation.

Repeat with a second coin.

Continue in this way until you have six coins, piled on top of one another, at the bottom of your imaginary well.

Now imagine yourself carrying out the stressful activity in a calm, confident and relaxed frame of mind. See it, hear it, touch and even taste it where appropriate.

If you start feeling stressed, return to the image of the gold coins and relax your mind again before returning to the stressful activity.

In time you'll find that any stress associated with performing this activity decreases. You may also want to experiment with different types of response on your own part, so as to rehearse a number of varying scenarios. Rehearsing in your imagination, while physically and mentally relaxed, makes them easier to cope with in real life.

Finish with a further period of soothing mental imagery.

Sensualisation is an excellent technique for dealing with potentially stressful confrontations and challenges only a few moments before they arise. If, for example, you have an appointment with a difficult client, sixty seconds of sensualisation should be sufficient to help you handle the meeting in a more relaxed, confident and effective manner.

30

Winding Down From Daily Stress

Many people bring their work stress home, leading to squabbles, fights, frustration and guilt. All of which, of course, produce even higher levels of stress.

In order to wind down from workplace stresses it is important to set aside some time for yourself soon after you get home. After carrying out one minute of deep-muscle relaxation to reduce physical tension, you will find it very helpful to spend a further short period – as little as sixty seconds can prove beneficial – in calming your mind.

One of the most powerful techniques for achieving inner tranquillity is meditation. Even a brief period of meditation is sufficient to create a barrier between work worries and home life. It also rebuilds depleted reserves of SRC, which can then be used to deal with any stressful family problems.

I know that this suggestion will raise doubts in the minds of many. Because of its supposed metaphysical associations, some people look on meditation as something connected with New Agers and eastern mysticism. In fact, meditation is no more than a technique for concentrating and calming the mind.

For others, meditation sounds difficult and time-consuming to learn. While I am not suggesting you can go and meditate successfully without any practice, the skill of brief meditation can be mastered fairly rapidly and easily.

As to its benefits, numerous studies have demonstrated that meditation acts as a potent antidote to stress. Dr Kenneth Eppley of Stanford University in California, who investigated the value of Transcendental Meditation, found it to be twice as effective in reducing anxiety as relaxation alone.

Research into the effects of meditation on people over eighty showed that those practising meditation had lowered their systolic blood-pressure from 140 to 128, had better memories and were capable of problem-solving more flexibly.

Another study, by Robert Wallace and Herbert Benson of Harvard Medical School, found that oxygen consumption dropped sharply during meditation and rose again only slowly afterwards. Blood-pressure remained low, while levels of muscle lactate declined sharply and continued to fall for a few minutes after the meditation. This finding is significant, because we experience a *rise* in lactate when stressed, and people with hypertension have consistently high lactate levels.

Heart-rate during meditation slows by an average of three beats per minute, while brain activity shows a marked increase in alpha waves, electrical patterns associated with a state of relaxed alertness.

Technique Thirty-Five: For Controlling Mental Stress

Sit down, half close your eyes and focus on a spot on the ground a few feet ahead.

If you meditate in the same place on a regular basis, you may find it helpful to place a coloured dot, about the size of a coin, on some part of the floor or low down on a wall. Suitable colours are yellow, blue or green, all of which assist in developing a relaxed mental state. If this is not possible, then stick a coloured dot on a small plain card and carry it with you. Place it on the floor immediately before you start to meditate. In addition to providing a consistent point of focus, using your own coloured dot will help you get into the habit of focusing your mind. After a time, it acts in somewhat the same way as the ringing bell used by Ivan Pavlov to make dogs salivate in anticipation of food. Here however your mind is anticipating psychological refreshment.

Breathe slowly and deeply while concentrating on the spot.

That's all you have to do.

For sixty seconds try not to pay attention to anything but that spot.

Thoughts and images will flash into and out of your mind. Let them. Develop a passive indifference towards all these distractions.

As you notice that your concentration is faltering, bring your mental focus gently back to the coloured dot. The main thing is never to think about what you are doing or worry that you may not be doing it quite right. As your skill improves, you'll find that distracting ideas intrude less and less frequently.

Your meditation complete, stand up slowly and try to carry those feelings of mental and physical relaxation through into the rest of your day. Use meditation whenever your mind becomes confused, distracted or disturbed.

Technique Thirty-Six: Active Meditation

Active Meditation means concentrating all your attention on the job at hand, no matter how menial.

While washing dishes, for example, you might focus on the colour of the soap bubbles, or the sensations of warm, soapy water on your hands.

While walking, spend sixty seconds focusing all your attention on the sights, sounds and smells around you. Scrutinise the shape and colour of buildings, plants, trees, the sky, clouds. Pay close attention to the noises of town or countryside. Sniff the wind. What scents does it carry?

By learning to focus your mind for brief periods in

this way, you will safeguard yourself against the stress of worrying thoughts. You will also start living in the 'here and now' rather than the past or the future, where so many spend so much of their waking hours.

Combating Stress in Specific Muscles

Deep-muscle relaxation will help reduce over-all stress. It may not, however, be sufficient to reduce stress in specific muscles that have been placed under undue tension during your working day. For instance, if you have been doing heavy lifting work, your arms and shoulders may be especially tense and stressed.

The following techniques should be used in addition to sixty seconds of general relaxation if you notice lingering stress in your:

> Forehead
> Jaw
> Shoulders
> Hands and arms
> Back

Technique Thirty-Seven: For Destressing Your Forehead

Your face is especially vulnerable to stress problems, because the muscles are so easily tensed. While concentrating, you may unknowingly be tensing the corrugator muscle, located above the nose, into a frown. Even this apparently trivial action will lead to an unnecessary expenditure of SRC.

An easy way to monitor corrugator-muscle tension is to place a length of sticky tape across your forehead. Now, each time you frown, the tape will tighten and provide immediate feedback. Use this simple device to identify those occasions when you automatically furrow your brow, such as reading, talking on the phone, concentrating on a problem, and so forth. You may be surprised at how much of a habit frowning has become. At such times make a conscious effort to smooth out your brow.

Deliberately tense the muscles by opening your eyes wide as though asking a question.

Now frown hard and screw up your eyes.

Hold this tension for a slow count to five, then relax.

Let your eyelids rest lightly together. Smooth out your brow.

Tension headaches can also be eased using massage (see Technique Nineteen) and by placing a cool, damp cloth over your brow.

Technique Thirty-Eight: For Destressing Your Jaw

Another common focus of facial tension is your jaw muscle, the masseter.

Since your jawbone, like every joint in the body, rests on pads of cartilage, constant pressure will eventually wear these pads away, causing considerable discomfort. Long before that, however, you are liable to have worn down your molars as a result of 'night grinding' – known medically as *bruxism* – which occurs particularly during sleep. Stress in your jaw can radiate outwards to produce head- or earache as well as the dull facial pain and tenderness which are symptoms of temporomandibular-joint disorders.

This exercise, developed at Columbia University, will ensure that the muscles and ligaments of your jaw remain free of needless stress. It also helps eliminate the pain caused by cramps and spasms of the jaw.

Slowly open your mouth, as wide as you comfortably can without forcing your jaw. Continue breathing slowly and calmly as you do so.

Exhale while slowly closing your mouth.

Lightly massage the muscles over the joints of the jaw, where it hinges on to the skull.

Repeat ten times.

Now place your fist beneath your chin and open your mouth against this slight resistance.

Repeat twelve times.

This exercise should provide rapid relief for discomfort caused by over-stressed jaws. However, should the pain, teeth-clenching or night grinding be severe, consult your dentist or doctor.

Technique Thirty-Nine: For Destressing Your Shoulders 1

Shoulder tension is a common stress-related problem, frequently associated with tightness in your neck muscles. Many people seem literally to 'carry the weight of the world on their shoulders'. They sit hunched behind the wheel of their car, when seated at a desk or watching television. They shrug their shoulders while talking and even use them to keep their ears warm in winter!

To avoid a build-up of stress keep your shoulders loose and relaxed.

If you feel tension rising, roll your shoulders with an exaggerated 'rowing' action.

Repeat three times, rolling them three times clockwise and three times anticlockwise.

Now shrug hard, drawing your shoulders up towards your ears.

Repeat three times.

Squeeze the shoulders together across your chest, then allow them to flop down.

Repeat three times.

Draw them back, attempting to touch your shoulder-blades together.

Repeat three times.

Finally, swing them backwards and forwards, while

keeping your hands hanging loosely at your sides. Regard your neck as a pivot around which the shoulders are allowed to shimmy, like a Turkish belly dancer in action.

Technique Forty: For Destressing Your Shoulders 2

Moist, rather than dry, heat is best for easing stressed shoulders, so take a shower or soak in a warm bath. Use a few drops of ylang-ylang, camomile, or lavender essential oils in the water.

After warming your shoulders in the bath or shower, place your left hand on the right shoulder and use a *petrissage* massage technique (see Chapter 20) on your muscles. Start at one side of your neck and proceed outwards to the upper arms, applying a firm pressure.

Grasping the large muscles of your upper arm (biceps and triceps), move them in a circular fashion.

If any muscles feel especially stressed and tense, rub them gently.

Now massage your left shoulder and arm using your right hand.

Technique Forty-One: For Destressing Your Wrists

Excessively stressed wrists are most likely if your job involves repetitive actions, such as typing, operating a computer, or driving a car or truck.

This type of strain can also occur after playing a sport such as golf, squash or tennis, which involve vigorous wrist movements.

This procedure comes from China and is called *Huen-sau*, or 'circling hands'. It not only banishes needless tension in your wrists, but helps make them more supple. You can perform it either sitting or standing.

Stretch out your right hand, thumb tucked in, wrist uppermost.

Bend your wrist back towards your forearm.

Now, holding your elbow as still as you can, rotate

your hand in a clockwise direction, *without allowing your arm to twist with your hand* (this is extremely important).

When you have rotated your hand as far as possible, hold that position for a couple of seconds. Then, very suddenly, make a fist and immediately afterwards relax the muscles in your hand and arm.

When you perform this action correctly you will feel tension in your wrist and the underside of the forearm. This is an indication that those muscles are being loosened and strengthened.

Now rotate your hand back to the starting point and repeat this movement three times.

Then do the same with your left hand.

Technique Forty-Two: For Destressing Your Hands and Arms

This should be used when your whole arm, from shoulder to fingertips, has become stressed and aching.

With your right hand, rub the length of your bare left arm, starting at the back of the hand and moving along the outside of the arm to the left shoulder, then back along the inside of the arm to the palm.

Do this briskly and smoothly while applying continuous pressure. End this stroke as if flicking drops of water from your fingertips.

Repeat six times before massaging your right arm with the left hand.

Stroke your hand and wrist with the palm of the other hand.

Pull along every finger from base to tip, finishing each stroke with a brisk snap.

Use your opposite thumb to massage the palm and wrist of your upturned hand, applying a firm, circular movement.

Turn your hand over and repeat, including the knuckles.

Stroke the back of each hand with the palm of the other.

Technique Forty-Three: For Destressing Your Back

Pain in the lower back is due mainly to muscle weakness, tightness or spasm. According to Dr Zeb Kendrick, Director of the Biokinetics Research Laboratory at Temple University, the lower back is the 'abused link' in the body.

Pain here can arise because of stress in the ankles, knees, hips or shoulders. High heels are a common cause of low-back pain among women, since they throw the body out of alignment.

Lie on your back on the floor, arms at your sides, knees bent and feet flat on the floor.

Pull in your stomach while flattening your spine against the floor so that there is no space between your back and the ground. Check this with your hand.

Release your stomach.

Repeat three times, keeping your breathing slow and regular.

Now raise your buttocks from the floor by contracting them and using your stomach muscles.

Repeat three times.

Bring your knees up to your chest, back flat on the ground. Place your arms around your knees and draw them in as close as possible. Bring your head up to meet your knees.

Repeat three times.

Staying in the same position, cross your legs at the ankles and grasp each foot, keeping your chin tucked in and your body completely relaxed. Rock back and forth for a few seconds.

Technique Forty-Four: Foot Massage for Restful Sleep 1

This is extremely effective in ensuring a good night's sleep. Use whichever of the three techniques described here proves most effective, or switch between them to introduce variety into this end-of-the-day stress reducer.

Press the fingers of either hand into the ball of your right foot. Use a firm, circular motion as if using a screwdriver.

Repeat with your instep.

Form a ring with your thumb and index finger. Place it over each toe in turn and pull your toe, using a wiggling motion.

Pinch the tip of each toe.

Rub your index finger between all your toes.

Smooth the depressions on either side of your Achilles tendon using an upward motion.

Pinch the heel three times.

Finish by grasping your right foot on either side, with both hands, thumbs overlapping at the toes. While pushing your fingers into your sole, simultaneously use the balls of your hands to smooth your foot forward from ankle to toes.

Repeat with your left foot.

Technique Forty-Five: Foot Massage for Restful Sleep 2

Sit down and place your right ankle over your left knee.

Holding the right foot in one hand, rub the entire sole with the fingers of your other hand using firm pressure.

Repeat with your left foot.

Technique Forty-Six: Foot Massage For Restful Sleep 3

Using the heel of your right hand, apply deep massage strokes while holding your right foot in your left hand.

Massage between your toes.

Pull your foot upward to stretch the muscles and tendons.

Repeat with your left foot.

These massage techniques, combined with muscle

relaxation, should help ensure a deep, restful sleep in which your body's SRC reserves can be fully replenished.

32

Preparing for a Stress-Free Tomorrow

End today by preparing for tomorrow.

A good way of doing this is to use a visualisation derived from eastern medicine and based on a belief in *chakras*.

Eastern tradition claims that our body possesses seven chakras, or energy centres, associated with the endocrine and nervous systems. Each has its own colour and is related to specific areas of the body.

Chakras are usually depicted as lotus flowers or wheels around the spine, indicating different levels of consciousness. The lowest level represents normal, everyday awareness, whilst the highest symbolises man's quest for spirituality.

The first, or 'root' chakra, located at the base of the spine, is associated with the adrenal glands and the colour red. Linked to our primitive fight-or-flight survival mechanism, it has a significant role in stress.

The second chakra, situated immediately above the genitals, is associated with sensations linked to taste, such as appetite and feelings. The sex chakra, it is associated with the colour orange.

Chakra three, found in the solar plexus, is our centre of personal power. This chakra is responsible for our 'gut feelings' about somebody or something. Its colour is yellow.

Our fourth chakra lies at the heart and serves to integrate the lower chakras into love and harmony. The colour of this chakra is green.

Chakra five, the throat chakra – associated with the thymus gland – is the chakra of self-expression. Its colour is blue.

The sixth chakra, linked to the endocrine system, is located at the centre of the forehead, and governs consciousness and awareness. Its colour is indigo.

The seventh, brain chakra, found at the top of the head, is linked to the pineal gland and nervous system. This represents the connection between the material and spiritual worlds. Its colour is violet.

When we are excessively stressed our distress shows itself in one of the parts of our body controlled by a particular chakra. A threat to psychological survival, which is often present in a stressful situation, affects our first chakra, causing damage to our adrenal glands and weakening the immune system.

Technique Forty-Seven: Replenishing Your Stress Resistance Reserves

This should be carried out last thing at night while sitting or lying in a comfortable and relaxed position.

Fix your attention on the first chakra at the base of your spine. Imagine the colour red, either as a red object – such as a dress, a car, a sunset – or as a diffuse red glow flowing into the lower part of your body.

After a few moments, shift attention to the second chakra in your genital region, and create the colour orange in your imagination. Again, use an orange-coloured object, such as a sunrise, or the diffuse image of orange, to suffuse this area of your body with colour.

Moving upwards to the third chakra, imagine a vivid yellow image filling and shimmering around your midriff.

Continue working your way through each of the chakras in this way, allowing their unique colour to flow into the appropriate area of your body.

The easiest way of remembering the colours is with the old schoolroom mnemonic:

*R*ichard *O*f *Y*ork *G*ave *B*attle *I*n *V*ain, for
'Red, Orange, Yellow, Green, Blue, Indigo, Violet'.

When you have reached your final chakra, imagine yourself surrounded by white light. Feel this light growing stronger and stronger, becoming clearer and clearer. Picture this vivid illumination as pure and healing.

Let the light flood over you, around you and through your entire body, penetrating every part of your being from the top of your head to the soles of your feet.

As the light flows through you, imagine it warming and soothing away any remaining stress or tensions.

Now go to sleep in a calm and relaxed state of mind and body, renewed by your visualisation.

Your reserves of Stress Resistance Currency are fully restored. You are ready to face whatever stresses tomorrow may bring – confidently, calmly and creatively.

33

Putting More Stress into Your Life

The risk of 'rust-out' caused by having insufficient stress in your life is less often recognised as a health hazard than the dangers of burn-out caused by excessive stress.

Neither managers nor individuals fully appreciate that being trapped into a boring, routine task can be as harmful to a person's mental and physical health as attempting to cope with too much change.

Most jobs, of course, involve a certain amount of routine and many goals can only be achieved provided one has sufficient self-discipline to master the more boring basics. When learning a foreign language or a musical instrument, for example, a great deal of rote learning and routine practice are essential.

The risk of rust-out increases sharply, however, when routine becomes an end in itself, when each and every day takes on the same predictable pattern.

Among the most likely victims of rust-out are:

> Production-line workers performing the same
>   actions, day in, day out, sometimes without
>   ever seeing the finished results of their labour
> Intelligent people obliged to earn their living in
>   jobs that do little or nothing to stretch them
>   mentally. Men and women whose intellectual
>   challenges are reduced to a few predictable
>   actions
> Women and (less often) men who give up a

stimulating career to raise a family and find
themselves trapped in a domestic routine

Previously active people forced into a life of
idleness by retirement. Although the first
months may prove a pleasant change from
being a slave to the nine-to-five, they
frequently find that leisure pursuits such as
golf or gardening, which they believed would
keep them stimulated, lose their appeal when
they are the only ways of passing time

Unfortunately, rust-out is often far harder for individuals to deal with than burn-out.

Whilst, as this book demonstrates, there are many
practical ways in which you can reduce stress in your
life, it is usually more difficult to make necessary changes
in an unstimulating lifestyle. This is especially true when
that dull routine is an essential part of your job.

Some companies, recognising the very real dangers of
mind-numbing production-line work, are taking positive
steps to improve manufacturing procedures.

One method is to rotate workers between routine jobs
while another is to create small production teams which
see a job through more or less from start to finish, a
technique pioneered by Volvo.

Although at a personal level your ability to improve
workplace practices is likely to be limited, there are still
ways of stimulating yourself by making changes in your
leisure-time activities. Here are six suggestions that you
may find useful:

One

Remove as many of the 'should's from your private
life as possible and replace them with 'want's.

If you are only doing something tedious because somebody else says you 'should' be doing it, consider whether
this is something you also *want* to do.

Do you get pleasure from the activity? Is it something

you look forward to or just another chore to be got through?

If, for example, you are attending an aerobics class you find boring because your partner says you 'should', find another way of keeping fit that you 'want' to do. The more wants and fewer shoulds that exist in your life, the more pleasantly stressed you will become.

Two

Where possible, delegate some of the chores you find boring to others who *want* to do them.

Mary loved baking but hated ironing. Joyce found ironing relaxing but couldn't stand cooking. So these neighbours swopped those jobs. In exchange for taking on Mary's weekly ironing Joyce now receives freshly baked cakes.

Philip, a self-employed car mechanic, hated doing his VAT returns yet was unable to afford the services of an accountant. Then he discovered that Tamsin, one of his customers, was a qualified bookkeeper. Now she does his VAT in return for having her car serviced.

Swopping routine jobs you hate for those you enjoy can be a great way of escaping tedious chores. One way to start such networking is by putting a card in your local newsagent's window or supermarket display board.

Three

Meet more people. Develop a fuller social life. Take part in local activities. Join clubs and societies in areas that specially interest you. But only if this is a 'want' not a 'should'.

Four

Challenge your brain. Like our body, the brain needs regular work-outs to remain in peak condition. Why not study at home? Either for pleasure, or as a way of gaining more qualifications, perhaps as a stepping stone to promotion or a more stimulating job.

Local authorities run a wide range of evening classes

and weekend courses, while for more serious study there is always the Open University.

Five

Take exercise. The more sluggish your system, the harder it is to summon enthusiasm for anything. Brisk exercise in the fresh air is an excellent antidote to boredom.

But don't fall into the trap of always taking the same type of exercise in the same location, for instance by always walking or jogging in the local park. If you do this it will rapidly turn into another tedious chore to be got through.

Vary the type of exercise and the location by walking – preferably in different settings – once or twice a week, swimming once a week, perhaps joining an aerobics class, attending keep-fit lessons, and so on.

Six

Be proactive in anticipating life changes, such as retirement or the time your children leave home, which will give you more free time.

Plan how you intend to fill those extra hours in the day. But do not make the mistake of assuming that any single activity is going to retain its interest if that is all you have planned to do.

Ten Golden Rules for Stress Management

The procedures for one-minute stress management that I have described in this book can only be of maximum benefit when used together with these golden rules.

Rule One: Never say never
Banish the words 'problem' and 'difficulty' from your vocabulary and replace them with 'challenge' and 'opportunity'.

Rule Two: Act on facts – not assumptions
Always try to make your decisions on the basis of facts rather than assumptions.

Acting impulsively on incomplete or inaccurate information only makes matters worse. If you are in the habit of sounding off without considering the consequences, visualise a large pot of glue, the kind used around offices and handicraft departments. Any time you feel tempted to speak first and think second, imagine gluing your lips together, making it impossible to blurt things out.

The same technique can be used to control anything from angry outbursts to jumping to conclusions. Picture that thought, word, or action daubed with glue and firmly sealed.

To be understood you must first understand. And this means really listening to what people are saying. Never assume you know what others are thinking. Ask them and listen to what they say. Not only to their words, but to the emotions lying behind those words.

Rule Three: Never generalise

Reject any thoughts that include words such as 'all', 'nothing', 'always', 'none', 'everybody', 'nobody'.

Comments such as 'I've always been a failure,' 'Nothing I have ever done is worthwhile,' 'Everybody enjoys life more than I do,' 'Nobody finds me attractive' are both unhelpful and stressful, undermining confidence and damaging self-esteem.

Rule Four: Accept your feelings

Never reject your emotions, even the painful ones. Feelings that are repressed or denied generate significant stress. If, for instance, you feel angry and upset, then allow those emotions expression. Not by becoming aggressive and attacking others, but by openly and honestly admitting them. If not to other people then at least to yourself.

Rule Five: Accept responsibility for yourself

Stop blaming others – parents, teachers, family, employer, friends or colleagues – for how your life is turning out.

Wherever you are, *you* got yourself there. Wherever you are going, *you* will be deciding the direction of your journey.

Walking without the crutches of dependency will be tough at first, but in time you will be so strong that such support is never again needed.

Rule Six: Abandon false hopes

Stop believing that some miracle is going to save you from your own laziness, folly, lack of confidence, low self-esteem or whatever else you regard as the root cause of current stress problems. Only *you* are in a position to shape your life for better or for worse. The sooner that fact is accepted the faster life improves.

Rule Seven: Step back from your problems

Try and distance yourself from your problems for a while, so as to get them into perspective.

When times are hard and you feel depressed, say to yourself: 'However bad things are now, all this will pass.' Try and project yourself a few months or years into the future. Picture yourself as you'd ideally like to be. Now consider what practical steps must be taken in order to turn that dream into reality.

Rule Eight: Simplify your lifestyle

Start dropping things you dislike and doing things you like. Slow the pace of your life. Do not try to cram quite so many things into it.

Reflect on your actions more carefully before agreeing to do something. Read less but read more slowly.

If you do not believe an activity is worth doing and you get no enjoyment from it, stop doing it.

Rule Nine: Spend time with nature

Even if you live in the heart of town, visit local parks and make regular trips into the countryside. You will relax more easily in natural surroundings.

Where possible, walk to work through a park or green open space instead of down city streets.

Grow herbs on your windowsill.

Decorate your room with pot-plants.

Make a meditation garden for your home or office. The most famous, Ryoan-ji in Kyoto, Japan, is simply a rectangle of sand a few feet square with fifteen carefully placed stones and some dark moss. Create your own in any suitably sized wooden box filled with sand or pebbles. Bring home a small piece of natural material, such as wind-smoothed wood, an interesting stone, a coloured shell, and make it a focus point while meditating.

Find a poster or even a postcard illustrating a beautiful natural scene.

Take your own colour photographs of a favourite countryside, mountain or seashore view.

When stress rises spend sixty seconds studying that relaxing scene. Imagine yourself in those tranquil surroundings. Close your eyes and attempt to re-create that tranquil image in your mind's eye.

As you do so, imagine the sounds, smells and any other sensations associated with the scene. The warmth of sunshine on your body, the freshness of a sea breeze, the pure air from snow-covered mountains.

When outdoors on a sunny day, shut your eyes and turn towards the sun for twenty seconds, making certain to keep your eyes tightly closed while doing so. Imagine the red glow on your eyelids penetrating your body, warming, relaxing and healing. Very gently massage your closed eyelids with your fingertips. When you open your eyes again you'll be amazed at how much sharper and brighter the colours around you appear.

If you spend a large part of each day doing close work, watching a computer screen, reading or writing, perform this exercise at least once every hour.

Glance up from the document or your display screen to any distant object, such as the view from your window or even the other end of a large office. Now look back at the screen or documents. Repeat this six times in order to exercise the muscles responsible for focusing the eyes. This will reduce eye strain and keep your eye muscles healthy.

Rule Ten: Make and take decisions with courage

Every decision you make is an opportunity to discover more about life. Each new path you follow opens fresh possibilities for your mental, physical and spiritual growth.

Accept responsibility for your choices.

If they turn out less well than you expected, take whatever practical steps are needed to change your situation.

Be flexible.

When faced with two paths to take through life, see both as offering opportunities for growth instead of viewing one as offering sure success and the other equally certain failure.

Each time you cope with a situation that previously made you fearful, your self-esteem increases. Once you realise that you can and will survive, no matter what, your fears are diminished.

Your Way Ahead

In my work as a psychologist I have seen many previously energetic and enthusiastic high achievers burned out by stress.

You can never escape from stress.

But you can learn to manage it.

By doing so you bring under control a potentially life-threatening force. A power capable of destroying your relationships, damaging your health and preventing you from enjoying the rewards of life you have striven so hard to achieve.

Yet a power which, when managed correctly, can also assist you in achieving your goals, safeguard your health and lead to even greater happiness and fulfilment.

The choice is yours.

A Full List of Cedar Books

While every effort is made to keep prices low, it is sometimes necessary to increase prices at short notice. Mandarin Paperbacks reserves the right to show new retail prices on covers which may differ from those previously advertised in the text or elsewhere.

The prices shown below were correct at the time of going to press.

☐	7493 0794 3	**Finding Love, Keeping Love**	Judith Sills £4.99
☐	7493 0526 6	**Coming Back**	Ann Kaiser Sterns £5.99
☐	7493 0936 9	**The Courage to Grieve**	Judith Tatelbaum £5.99
☐	7493 0718 8	**Seeds of Greatness**	Denis Waitley £4.99
☐	7493 1210 6	**Divorce Hangover**	Anne Walther £5.99
☐	7493 1049 9	**Irritable Bowel Syndrome**	Geoff Watts £5.99

All these books are available at your bookshop or newsagent, or can be ordered direct from the publisher. Just tick the titles you want and fill in the form below.

Mandarin Paperbacks, Cash Sales Department, PO Box 11, Falmouth, Cornwall TR10 9EN.

Please send cheque or postal order, no currency, for purchase price quoted and allow the following for postage and packing:

UK including
BFPO
£1.00 for the first book, 50p for the second and 30p for each additional book ordered to a maximum charge of £3.00.

Overseas
including Eire
£2 for the first book, £1.00 for the second and 50p for each additional book thereafter.

NAME (Block letters) ....

ADDRESS...

....

☐ I enclose my remittance for ....

☐ I wish to pay by Access/Visa Card Number

Expiry Date